CW01403491

Dear Jan & [...]
       Family,
Have a lovely X-mas
& best wishes for
a happy 1999
Lots of love,
    Emma

(X-mas '98)

Family Ties

Family Ties

Australian Poems of the Family

Edited by Jennifer Strauss

Melbourne

OXFORD UNIVERSITY PRESS

Oxford   Auckland   New York

This project has been assisted by the Commonwealth Government through the Australia Council, its arts funding and advisory body.

OXFORD UNIVERSITY PRESS AUSTRALIA

Oxford New York
Athens Auckland Bangkok Bogota Bombay
Buenos Aires Calcutta Cape Town Dar es Salaam
Delhi Florence Hong Kong Istanbul Karachi
Kuala Lumpur Madras Madrid Melbourne
Mexico City Nairobi Paris Port Moresby
Singapore Taipei Tokyo Toronto Warsaw
and associated companies in
Berlin Ibadan

OXFORD is a trade mark of Oxford University Press

National Library of Australia
Cataloguing-in-publication data:

   Family ties: Australian poems of the family.
   Includes index.
   ISBN 0 19 553789 0.
   1. Australian poetry – 20th century.
   2. Family – Australia – poetry.
   I. Strauss, Jennifer, 1933– .
   A821.3080355

Edited by Cathryn Game
Text and cover designed by Anitra Blackford
Typeset by Solo Typesetting
Printed by Kyodo
Published by Oxford University Press
253 Normanby Road, South Melbourne, Australia

CONTENTS

INTRODUCTION

'The sad geometry of family love': in that final line of 'Father, Mother, Son' by James McAuley lies the origin of this anthology. I was selecting McAuley's poem for *The Oxford Book of Australian Love Poems*, but it struck me that its conclusion would make a good epigraph for an anthology of family poems. I wondered, though, whether they would all turn out to be quietly desperate, or perhaps angry, or sentimental—alternative versions, if not of McAuley, then of Philip Larkin's 'They fuck you up, your mum and dad' ('This be the verse') or of 'Home Sweet Home'. Certainly some of these poems represent pathologies of the family, if not with Larkin's calculated crudity; but they must be weighed against those that celebrate it. And among the celebratory poems, Les Murray's teasingly titled 'Home Suite' makes a connection that is primary to many:

> First home as last
> is a rounded way to live
> but to tell another You're my home
> speaks of a greater love.

The house as the *locus* of the family, not merely a setting but somehow an integral part of its life, is a motif that returns again and again. John Blight may remind readers of 'Houses and Homes' that 'there is/distinction between a house and a home', and assert, as Murray does, that the love between family members is the essence of home. Memories of houses (and of household objects) remain, however, profoundly entangled with family experiences in poems like Jennifer Rankin's 'Daub Wall', Thomas Shapcott's 'Instructions for Moving', Rhyll McMaster's 'Holiday House', Tracy Ryan's 'Morningswood', or Inez Hyland's engaging defence in 'Disloyalty' of that most Australian of first homes, the bush hut. And in a collection of Australian family poems, it would be surprising not to find representation of two characteristic sites of family activity: verandahs (Jean Kent) and backyards (John Tranter). With such a strong presence of the family home, it seemed appropriate that the collection should end with Jemal Sharah's poem, 'The Lares', about that household guardian, the dog—although (and rather to my surprise), cats had proved a far more frequent focus of poetic attention.

It is, of course, more common in our society to define families by their relationship with other people than by their relationship with place, although a poem like Jack Davis's 'The First-born' reminds us that, for Australia's indigenous people, the primary kin relationship is with the land. Houses for them are likely to be irrelevant, or to be associated, for urbanised Aboriginals like the speaker of Graeme Dixon's 'To Let', with exclusion and rejection.

A number of poems in this anthology, however, have been chosen to stretch the idea of 'family' relationships. One such group stresses human kinship with the animal world. In the extract from James Michael's 'John Cumberland', kinship with animals is a benign source of 'pure' emotions' aroused in the child by stories of 'lambs lost in the snow'. John Shaw Neilson's 'The Vixen has Spoken' is a darker poem, a disturbing reminder that one aspect of such kinship is that both humans and animals kill (lambs) to survive.

A more idealistic extended category of the family is one often characterised as 'the family of man', represented in the political terms of Charles Harpur's 'A Man Shall Be a Man Yet', in the pragmatic kindliness of the poor in Mary Fullerton's 'The Folk of Brenan's Lane', and in the more specific form of the family (or brotherhood) of artists in Henry Kendall's 'In Memoriam: Daniel Henry Deniehy'. That such wider social affiliations can come into conflict with more immediate family ties, rather than reinforcing them, is tellingly realised in Mary Gilmore's 'Nationality':

> All men at God's round table sit,
> And all men must be fed;
> But this loaf in my hand,
> This is my son's bread.

The majority of poems in the collection do, in fact, deal with those more immediate relationships that we think of as constituting the family. As subjects, grandparents abound—and an occasional more remote ancestor, as in R.D. Fitzgerald's 'The Wind at Your

Door'—but grandchildren are scarce. There are numerous parents, even a few parents-in-law; lots of children but rather fewer spouses and siblings; a sprinkling of uncles and aunts, nieces and nephews; not many cousins. The latter actually figured in one of those crises of choice to which anthologists are subject. David Campbell's splendid sequence 'Death and Pretty Cousins' seemed an obvious choice; but its length would have engrossed all the space available for his work, given my decision that the anthology should cover a broad spectrum of poets. A cost of this decision was the difficulty of selecting examples from those poets who, like Campbell, had written a large number of relevant poems—notably Mary Gilmore, Henry Lawson, Judith Wright, Gwen Harwood, Dorothy Hewett, Peter Porter, Bruce Dawe, Fay Zwicky, Les Murray, Geoffrey Lehmann, Robert Adamson, and Rhyll McMaster.

In the event, I was influenced to choose other Campbell poems by two facts: that I could not resist 'The Australian Dream', and that he had very recently been represented by 'Death and Pretty Cousins' in Peter Porter's *Oxford Book of Modern Australian Verse*. It is, of course, not feasible to avoid all overlap with existing anthologies, but when poems are of equal merit and relevance, the interests of both poet and readers are best served by choosing those less frequently anthologised. Poets very naturally do not want to be known for only one or two poems. This alone would have been enough to deflect me from Gwen Harwood's 'In the Park', even if it had not been crowded out by other choices. Her triumphant affirmation of motherhood in 'An Impromptu for Ann Jennings', and two fine elegies, one for a stillborn daughter ('Dialogue'), the other for the 'Mother Who Gave Me Life', had been in my mind from the beginning. These poems provide a balance to the general preponderance of elegies for fathers, notably the sequences 'Stroke' by Vincent Buckley and 'Evening at Bunyah' by Les Murray.

For all the variety of experiences and attitudes exhibited in these poems, the family emerges as an institution with a remarkably tenacious hold not only on the way life is organised practically but also on the way it is imagined and valued. Positive representations maintain a steady presence in the face of negative perceptions. It was not surprising to find, in poets like Gillian Hanscombe and Alan

Wearne, examples of the 1960s rebellion against the very idea of the nuclear family, but the negativity of some poems from an earlier period was unexpected. Few poems were as sweepingly dismissive of domesticity as Brennan's romantic Wanderer, but both male and female poets wrote of experiencing the presence of the family as constraint (e.g. Lawson's 'My Father-in-Law and I') and its absence as freedom rather than deprivation (e.g. Victor Daley's 'An Australian Bachelor's Soliloquy', Elsie Cole's 'Fenella West', and Mary Finnin's 'Mad Lucy'). The breaking up of the family through divorce, glimpsed briefly and bitterly in Lawson's late poems, is of course a more modern theme. Edith Speers treats the dissolution of an unsatisfactory relationship with relish, but this attitude is far less typical than the sadness of Geoffrey Lehmann's 'The Flight of Children', Kate Llewellyn's 'Divorce', or David Reiter's 'Cats Slip In', although sadness is modulated with a certain wryness in the last two.

Given this centrality of the family, it is worth reminding ourselves that Australian history began with the breaking of families. It seemed only right to begin this anthology with a poem that commemorates one aspect of that destruction: Harpur's 'An Aboriginal Mother's Lament'. Poems by early convicts and settlers, however, spoke more of exile from homeland than loss of family. It was in 'Letter Home (Mary Talbot)', the 1997 work of Jordie Albiston, that I finally found a matching historical piece, a poem of the broken family life of a convict woman.

For the past fifty or so years, however, we have been hearing other accounts of broken or traumatised families in the poems of immigrant writers. In these poems, families are not necessarily divided by the physical distance that separates Mary Talbot from her child: they may be separated by an incommensurable gulf of experience between parents and children, as in Lily Brett's *Auschwitz Poems*, but they are also separated by the breaking of the bond of a common language. The joyful entry into language that is Chris Wallace-Crabbe's in 'Inheritance' is problematic or denied to the children in Silvana Gardner's 'Forbidden Language' or Tom Petsinis's *Inheritance*.

It has been difficult enough to decide which poems to mention in this introduction. It was much harder to decide which poems must be eliminated from the more than three hundred that remained as those I really wanted to include after several rounds of culling from the bulging file of possibilities. And again, as with *Love Poems*, some excellent poets are not represented here, simply because their thematic interests happen to lie elsewhere, while some poems would have been included here if they had not already found a place in that earlier collection. Love and the family are not easily disentangled. There will surely also be poems that I have simply missed seeing, even in two years of searching.

Much of my two years of research was made possible by an Australian Research Council Grant, which enabled me to employ Joy McEntee as a very able research assistant, accurate in record-keeping, patient with endless photocopying, and enthusiastic and determined in pursuit of elusive copies of slim volumes and likely poems. My thanks go to her and the ARC, and to Peter Rose of Oxford University Press for his support in seeing this project through a lengthy period of gestation.

Charles Harpur
An Aboriginal Mother's Lament

It will be remembered by many Colonists, that about five and twenty years ago (dating back from 1867) a party of Stockmen (several of whom were afterwards hanged for the crime) made wholesale slaughter of a small tribe of defenceless Blacks—to the number, it is believed, of more than forty;—heaping their bodies, as they butchered them like cattle, upon a large fire kindled for the purpose. Of this doomed tribe, one woman only, with her infant, as it appeared subsequently from the evidence in the case, escaped the Whiteman's vengeance. And the Poem is supposed to describe the grief and despair of this Mother, after she has fled to a considerable distance from the scene of the massacre, and when wearied and overtaken by the night. C.H.

Still farther would I fly, my Child,
    To make thee safer yet,
From the Whiteman's so unsparing
    Dread hand, all murder-wet!—
Yet bear thee on as I have borne
    With stealthy strides wind-fleet,
But the dark shuts up the Forest,
    And thorns are in my feet!

O moan not! I would give this braid
    That once bound Hibbi's brow,
Were it but for a single palmful
    Of water for thee now.

Ah! spring not to his name;—no more
    To glad us may he come!
He is smouldering into ashes
    Beneath the blasted gum!
All charred and blasted by the fire
    The Whiteman kindled there,
And fed with our slaughtered kindred
    Till heaven-high went its glare!

O moan not! I would give this braid
  That once bound Hibbi's brow,
Were it but for a single palmful
  Of water for thee now.

And but for thee, I would their fire
  Had eaten me as fast!
Hark!—hark! do I hear *his* death-cry
  Yet lengthening up the blast?
But no—when his bound hands had signed
  The way that we should fly,
On the roaring pyre flung bleeding,
  I saw thy Father die!

O moan not! I would give this braid
  That once bound Hibbi's brow,
Were it but for a single palmful
  Of water for thee now.

No more shall his loud tomahawk
  Be plied to win our cheer,
Or the shining fish-pools darken
  Beneath his shadowing spear!
The fading tracks of his fleet foot
  Shall guide not as before,
And the mountain Spirits mimic
  His hunting call no more!

O moan not! I would give this braid,
  Thy Father's gift to me,
Were it but for a single palmful
  Of water now for thee!

A Man Shall be a Man Yet

It must be in Man's fortunes,
  Since the Sire of Man is God,
That a better ruler's coming
  Than grim Force with iron rod;
And to make our faith the firmer,

There is, even now, a great
And growing brotherhood of men
　Vow'd to that better state:
And whose standard is *that* standard
　'Neath whose broad folds unfurled
A man shall be a man yet
　All over the world.

Oh, then away for ever
　With all unfraternal hate—
All envyings 'twixt the rich and poor,
　The little and the great!
And be we of that noble
　And for ever growing band,
Whose worship is the Just and True
　Alike in every land:
And whose standard is *that* standard
　'Neath whose broad folds unfurled,
A man shall be a man yet
　All over the world.

But down with all down pullers—
　All mere haters of command!
For who bows not to what's noble
　And thence glorious in the land,
Can never be one in spirit
　With that fraternising host,
Which yet, in God's good time, is doomed
　To rule the social roost:
And whose standard is *that* standard
　'Neath whose broad folds unfurled,
A man shall be a man yet
　All over the world.

Down too with all mere brawlers
　At what luxury they see,
Since 'tis well to roll in riches
　If but fairly won they be—

Well to shine amongst our fellows,
    Though the thorough man alone
Is one who through his *golden heart*,
    And not his gold is known.
And whose standard is *that* standard
    'Neath whose broad folds unfurled,
A man shall be a man yet
    All over the world.

James Michael
From *John Cumberland*

My earliest memory is of a seat
    On a low footstool, by a winter fire,
      Listening, while warm and ruddy with its glow,
      To stories of the lambs lost in the snow,
    Stories of which I never seem'd to tire,
Although they made my heart so sadly beat:
And, somehow, the impression was profound
    Young as I was; for, to this very day,
      It stirs my inmost heart to hear a lamb
      Lift up a piteous crying for its dam,
    And all my soul leaps back upon its way,
And falls upon its childhood at the sound,
And paints her there, my Mother, gentle-ey'd,
    And quiet voiced, and with a long thin hand;
      Telling the story in the twilight hour,
      While I sat rapt and awestruck, till a shower
Of tears reliev'd me—I have paced life's sand,
The barren sand of life, since then, in pride
That weeps but seldom for another's woe,
    Though freely for its own—I have not shed
      Too many tears. None, I am sure, like those
      Unselfish, scalding, bitter drops, that rose
Out of my simple childhood. They are dead,
These child-emotions. Never shall I know

Others so pure; until, from mortal stain,
   Wash'd angel-white in the celestial river,
    A purer lamb, who bled to set me free,
    By His own mighty grace, deliver me,
   Wipe pride out of my heart again for ever,
And make me like a little child again.

Henry Kendall
In Memoriam Daniel Henry Deniehy

Take the harp, but very softly for our brother touch the strings:
Wind and wood shall help to wail him, waves and mournful
   mountain-springs.
Take the harp, but very softly, for the friend who grew so old
Through the hours we would not hear of—nights we would not
   fain behold!
Other voices, sweeter voices, shall lament him year by year,
Though the morning finds us lonely, though we sit and marvel
   here:
Marvel much while Summer cometh trammelled with
   November wheat,
Gold about her forehead gleaming, green and gold about her
   feet;
Yea, and while the land is dark with plover, gull, and gloomy
   glede,
Where the cold swift songs of Winter fill the interlucent reed.

Yet my harp, and O, my fathers, never look for Sorrow's lay,
Making life a mighty darkness in the patient noon of day;
Since he resteth whom we loved so, out beyond these fleeting
   seas,
Blowing clouds, and restless regions paved with old perplexities,
In a land where thunder breaks not, in a place unknown of
   snow,
Where the rain is mute for ever, where the wild winds never go;
Home of far-forgotten phantoms—genii of our peaceful prime,
Shining by perpetual waters past the ways of Change and Time:

Haven of the harried spirit, where it folds its wearied
    wings,
Turns its face and sleeps a sleep with deep forgetfulness of
    things.
His should be a grave by mountains, in a cool and
    thick-mossed lea,
With the lone creek falling past it—falling ever to the sea.

His should be a grave by waters, by a bright and broad
    lagoon,
Making steadfast splendours hallowed of the quiet shining
    moon.
There the elves of many forests—wandering winds and
    flying lights—
Born of green, of happy mornings, dear to yellow summer
    nights,
Full of dole for him that loved them, then might halt, and
    then might go,
Finding fathers of the people to their children speaking
    low—
Speaking low of one who, failing, suffered all the poet's
    pain,
Dying with the dead leaves round him—hopes which
    never grow again.

Araluen

Take this rose and very gently place it on the tender, deep
Mosses where our little darling Araluen, lies asleep.
Put the blossom close to baby—kneel with me, my love,
    and pray;
We must leave the bird we've buried—say goodbye to her
    today.
In the shadow of our trouble, we must go to other lands;
And the flowers we have fostered will be left to other
    hands.
Other eyes will watch them growing—other feet will
    softly tread

Where two hearts are nearly breaking: where so many tears are
   shed.
Bitter is the world we live in: life and love are mixed with
   pain—
We will never see these daisies; never water them again.

Ah, the saddest thought in leaving baby in this bush alone
Is that we have not been able on her grave to place a stone!
We have been too poor to do it; but, my darling, never mind!
God is in the gracious heavens, and his sun and rain are kind.
They will dress the spot with beauty, they will make the grasses
   grow:
Many winds will lull our birdie—many songs will come and go.
Here the blue-eyed Spring will linger—here the shining month
   will stay
Like a friend by Araluen, when we two are far away;
But, beyond the wild wide waters, we will tread another shore:
We will never watch this blossom—never see it any more.

Girl, whose hand at God's high altar in the dear dead year I
   pressed,
Lean your stricken head upon me: this is still your lover's breast!
She who sleeps was first and sweetest—none we have to take
   her place!
Empty is the little cradle, absent is the little face.
Other children may be given; but this rose beyond recall—
But this garland of your girlhood will be dearest of them all.
None will ever, Araluen, nestle where you used to be,
In my heart of hearts, you darling, when the world was new to
   me.
We were young when you were with us. Life and Love were
   happy things
To your father and your mother ere the angels gave you wings.

You that sit and sob beside me—you upon whose golden head
Many rains of many sorrows have from day to day been shed—
Who, because your love was noble, faced with me the lot
   austere

Ever pressing with its hardship on the man of letters here—
Let me feel that you are near me: lay your hand within mine
   own.
You are all I have to live for, now that we are left alone.
Three there were but one has vanished. Sins of mine have made
   you weep;
But forgive your baby's father now that baby is asleep.
Let us go, for night is falling—leave the darling with her
   flowers:
Other hands will come and tend them—other friends, in other
   hours.

Ada Cambridge
An Old Maid's Lament

Every wild she-bird has nest and mate in the warm April
            weather,
         But a captive woman, made for love—nor nest, nor
            mate has she.
In the spring of young desire, young men and maids are wed
            together,
         And the happy mothers flaunt their bliss for all the
            world to see.
Life's great sacramental feast for them—an empty board for me.

I, a young maid once, an old maid now, deposed, despised,
            forgotten—
         I, like them, have thrilled with passion and have
            dreamed of nuptial rest,
Of the trembling life within me of my baby unbegotten,
         Of the breathing new-born body to my yearning bosom
            prest—
         Of the rapture of its little soft mouth drinking at my
            breast.

Time, that heals so many sorrows, keeps mine ever freshly
            aching,

Though my face is growing furrowed and my brown hair
    turning white.
Still I mourn my irremidiable loss, asleep or waking—
    Still I hear my child's voice calling 'Mother' in the dead
        of night,
    And am haunted by those sweet eyes that will never see
        the light.

O my baby that I might have had! My darling, lost for ever!
    O the goodly years that might have been—now desolate
        and bare!
O malignant God or Fate, what have I done that I should never
        Take my birthright like the others, take the crown that
            women wear,
    And possess the common heritage to which all flesh is heir?

Louisa Lawson
A Pound a Mile

The tar-boy looked perplexed to see
    Tom Dawson cut the skin,
And Sweeper Bill remarked that he
    Had nothing in the bin.

His eyes for want of sleep were red,
    And slow his shears did click,
And whispers went around the shed
    That Dawson's wife was sick.

Then kindly spoke old Daddy Tonk:
    'Don't look so glum, my lad;
Is she, your missus, very cronk?'
    'Yes, mate,' said Tom, 'she's—bad.'

'Are there no women on the place?
    There should be two or three.'
'There are, but in my poor wife's case
    They say they're "all at sea".'

'Then bring a doctor,' Daddy said;
   'Don't let the woman die!'
But Tommy Dawson hung his head
   And made him no reply.

'Get Pile to come out if you can,
   He'll pull the missus through.
Spend all you have to save her, man,
   I would if I were you.'

Then Dawson looked up from the ground,
   And white his features grew:
'Look, mate! If you had not a pound
   Now tell me what you'd do?'

'What would it cost then, now, to send
   And fetch out Dr Pile?
Some of the men the cash would lend.'
   Tom groaned, 'A pound a mile.'

'That's stiff, by God!' said Monty Styles,
   'The doctor does it brown;
There's sixty-five, I know, good miles
   Between us and the town.'

'It is a "coo-ey" with her now,'
   Said Dawson, in despair.
'I cannot save her anyhow—
   I'm euchred everywhere.'

Then up sprang Maori, on the job—
'Here, look, see! There's my quid.
And here, look, see! So help me bob!
   There's two from Dick and Syd.'

And in his hat the money fell
   From willing hands and free.
'A quid a mile,' said Barney Bell;
   'Here goes! I'll give yer three.'

The Boss said, 'Put me down for ten,
    And catch the blood mare, Ted—
And put her in the sulky then—
    Don't wait till she is fed.

'Now, wire the doctor, quick, to come,
    And meet me mile for mile;
And, Tommy, man, hold up, old chum.'
    (Poor Tommy tried to smile.)

The squatter lit his pipe with care
    And drew his chin-strap in,
Then took his seat and touched the mare
    And started for the spin.

Then slow the hours of night went by
    To those around the shed,
For not a man had closed an eye
    Not one had gone to bed.

'She's sinking now,' the women said,
    'She can't much longer last;
Before an hour she will be dead,
    Her strength is failing fast.'

'I'll go and let the sliprails down,'
    The black boy slowly said,
For far along the road to town
    He heard a horse's tread.

Then everyone sprang up and bent
    A watchful eye and ear,
And soon the boss a 'coo-ey' sent
    To show that he was near.

Then in the middle of the night
    The blood mare, limping, came
All tucked and blown, and wet and white,
    And panting hard, but game.

The doctor quick and silently
    Then with the women went,
And very soon a baby's cry
    Was heard in Dawson's tent.

'Thank God,' he said, 'My work is done,'
    As Tommy's hand he pressed;
'I've saved your wife and little son,
    Let Nature do the rest.'

And then they went into the shed—
    The men and Dr Pile—
And drank his health in Queensland red,
    And paid him—pound for mile.

Victor Daley

The Australian Bachelor's Soliloquy, by a Jealous Married Man

The world goes well—goes very well with me;
I would not wish a better world to see.
Vain luxury I always did despise,
For, like Dan Horace, I would symbolize
The loveliness of life in figures fair—
Tobacco, claret, and an easy chair.
Vain luxury in me no chord can strike,
But this is comfort—this is what I like.
I am no Sybarite whose rose-leaf curled
Beneath him makes him quarrel with the world,
But just a single man—my own sole lord—
And this is, as it should be, my reward.

There are my pipes reposing in the rack,
Meerschaum and briar, golden-brown and black—
I still prefer a pipe to a cigar—
And yonder is my quaint tobacco jar,

A piece of Dresden pottery unique:
A workman's family might live a week
On what is costs, I hear, but, if they could,
The world would be no better, if as good.

There are my books—the books I love, encased
In noble Kelmscott binding, rich but chaste.
There is my Flaccus—bard who never bores—
The Patron Poet of wise Bachelors.
At times I hear him, in the stillness fine
Singing between his covers, like old wine
That murmurs in its cask of summers gone
And golden suns that on its birthplace shone.

What have I lost? The dear domestic joys!
A howling horde of hungry girls and boys;
A wife made sour by constant motherhood,
A ceaseless struggle to buy clothes and food,
The need to keep a face of haggard cheer
Before the world from dismal year to year;—
The voice that once was musical and low
Grown shrill and acid as the sound a bow
Gone dry makes on an untuned violin;
The grace that pleased—when I was still to win—
And all the charming coquetry of dress
Debased to slippers, wrappers, dowdiness;—
The squalid fear I never felt before
To hear the landlord knocking at the door—
They say 'tis like the knocking in Macbeth,
And dreadful as the call of sudden Death;—
And when I have grown grey with years of strife,
Ungrateful children and a wizened wife...
He may who will—but I shall never be
The Haggard Father of a Family.

Here I can sit at ease on days of rain,
And read my Rabelais and my Montaigne,

Self-centred as a solitary star
That has no satellites its peace to mar.
Society salutes me with salaam,
For I am single—thank the Lord I am!

Inez Hyland
Disloyalty

Written on the occasion of H.R.H. the Duke of Edinburgh's visit
to —— Station.

Pull down the old hut, d'ye say, girls,
    That H.R.H. shan't see
The common place that used to do,
    Years by, for your mother and me?

No!—not for a dozen Princes,
    Nor lords nor dukes beside,
Will I pull down the poor old hut,
    Where your mother lived and died.

Oh, I know that it's old and crazy,
    I know that it's shabby and mean;
But it's going to stand as it is, girls,
    And I *won't* erect a screen

To shut out the rambling shingle hut
    From sight of this handsome place.
I should feel as if I had closed
    The door in your mother's face.

So if H.R.H. don't like that hut
    Himself and his lordly pack
May hump their blueys and go their way
    Out on the wallaby track.

A. B. Paterson
The Man Who was Away

The widow sought the lawyer's room with children three in tow,
She told the lawyer man her tale in tones of deepest woe.
She said, 'My husband took to drink for pains in his inside,
And never drew a sober breath from then until he died.

'He never drew a sober breath, he died without a will,
And I must sell the bit of land the childer's mouths to fill.
There's some is grown and gone away, but some is childer yet,
And times is very bad indeed—a livin's hard to get.

'There's Min and Sis and little Chris, they stops at home with
    me,
And Sal has married Greenhide Bill that breaks for Bidgeree.
And Fred is drovin' Conroy's sheep along the Castlereagh
And Charley's shearin' down the Bland, and Peter is away.'

The lawyer wrote the details down in ink of legal blue—
'There's Minnie, Susan, Christopher, they stop at home with
    you;
There's Sarah, Frederick, and Charles, I'll write to them today,
But what about the other son—the one who is away?

'You'll have to furnish his consent to sell the bit of land.'
The widow shuffled in her seat, 'Oh, don't you understand?
I thought a lawyer ought to know—I don't know what to say—
You'll have to do without him, boss, for Peter is away.'

But here the little boy spoke up—said he, 'We thought you
    knew;
He's done six months in Goulburn gaol—he's got six more to
    do.'
Thus in one comprehensive flash he made it clear as day,
The mystery of Peter's life—the man who was away.

A Bush Christening

On the outer Barcoo where the churches are few,
    And men of religion are scanty,
On a road never cross'd 'cept by folk that are lost
    One Michael Magee had a shanty.

Now this Mike was the dad of a ten-year-old lad,
    Plump, healthy, and stoutly conditioned;
He was strong as the best, but poor Mike had no rest
    For the youngster had never been christened.

And his wife used to cry, 'If the darlin' should die
    Saint Peter would not recognize him.'
But by luck he survived till a preacher arrived,
    Who agreed straightaway to baptize him.

Now the artful young rogue, while they held their collogue,
    With his ear to the keyhole was listenin';
And he muttered in fright, while his features turned white,
    'What the divil and all is this christenin'?'

He was none of your dolts—he had seen them brand colts,
    And it seemed to his small understanding,
If the man in the frock made him one of the flock,
    It must mean something very like branding.

So away with a rush he set off for the bush,
    While the tears in his eyelids they glistened—
''Tis outrageous,' says he, 'to brand youngsters like me;
    I'll be dashed if I'll stop to be christened!'

Like a young native dog he ran into a log,
    And his father with language uncivil,
Never heeding the 'praste', cried aloud in his haste
    'Come out and be christened, you divil!'

But he lay there as snug as a bug in a rug,
    And his parents in vain might reprove him,
Till his reverence spoke (he was fond of a joke)
    'I've a notion,' says he, 'that'll move him.

'Poke a stick up the log, give the spalpeen a prog;
    Poke him aisy—don't hurt him or maim him;
'Tis not long that he'll stand, I've the water at hand,
    As he rushes out this end I'll name him.

'Here he comes, and for shame! ye've forgotten the name—
    Is it Patsy or Michael or Dinnis?'
Here the youngster ran out, and the priest gave a shout—
    'Take your chance, anyhow, wid "Maginnis!"'

As the howling young cub ran away to the scrub
    Where he knew that pursuit would be risky,
The priest, as he fled, flung a flask at his head
    That was labelled 'Maginnis's Whisky'!

Now Maginnis Magee has been made a J.P.,
    And the one thing he hates more than sin is
To be asked by the folk, who have heard of the joke,
    How he came to be christened Maginnis!

Mary Gilmore
Marri'd

It's singin' in an' out,
    An' feelin' full of grace;
Here 'n' there, up an' down,
    An' round about th' place.

It's rollin' up your sleeves,
    An' whit'nin' up the hearth,
An' scrubbin' out th' floors,
    An' sweepin' down th' path;

It's bakin' tarts an' pies,
    An shinin' up th' knives;
An' feelin' 's if some days
    Was worth a thousand lives.

It's watchin' out th' door,
    An' watchin' by th' gate;

An' watchin' down th' road,
   An' wonderin' why he's late;

An' feelin' anxious-like,
   For fear there's something wrong;
An' wonderin' why he's kep',
   An' why he takes so long.

It's comin' back inside
   An' sittin' down a spell,
To sort o' make believe
   You're thinkin' things is well.

It's gettin' up again
   An' wand'rin' in an' out;
An' feelin' wistful-like,
   Not knowin' what about;

An' flushin' all at once,
   An' smilin' just so sweet,
An' feelin' real proud
   The place is fresh an' neat.

An' feelin' awful glad
   Like them that watch'd Silo'm;
An' everything because
   A man is comin' Home!

The Square Peg and the Round

When John McCosh went on the spree
He left his wife at home;
Said he, 'The Lord, He made man free,
And gave him leave to roam;
The Lord was very wise,' said he—
And blew upon the foam.

'The Lord was wise, and more than wise,
When He made human kind—
For one the road where'er it lies,
And one to stay behind;

For one to chase the hour that flies,
And one to sheaf and bind.

'The Lord was very wise,' he said,
And leaned above his beer,
And every loafer raised his head,
That he might better hear;
'For what,' said he, 'were women bred,
But for man's help and cheer!'

But all night long the woman watched,
Afraid at every sound;
And, as she sat, she sewed and patched,
And darned each rent she found;
And maybe wondered who had matched
The square peg with the round.

War

Out in the dust he lies;
    Flies in his mouth,
Ants in his eyes...

I stood at the door
    Where he went out;
Full-grown man,
    Ruddy and stout;

I heard the march
    Of the trampling feet,
Slow and steady
    Come down the street;

The beat of the drum
    Was clods on the heart,
For all that the regiment
    Looked so smart!

I heard the crackle
    Of hasty cheers

Run like the breaking
    Of unshed tears,

And just for a moment,
    As he went by,
I had sight of his face,
    And the flash of his eye.

He died a hero's death,
    They said,
When they came to tell me
    My boy was dead;

But out in the street
    A dead dog lies;
Flies in his mouth,
    Ants in his eyes.

Nationality

I have grown past hate and bitterness,
I see the world as one;
But though I can no longer hate,
My son is still my son.

All men at God's round table sit,
And all men must be fed;
But this loaf in my hand,
This loaf is my son's bread.

Henry Lawson
The Fire at Ross's Farm

The squatter saw his pastures wide
    Decrease, as one by one
The farmers moving to the west
    Selected on his run;
Selectors took the water up
    And all the black soil round;

The best grass-land the squatter had
    Was spoilt by Ross's Ground.

Now many schemes to shift old Ross
    Had racked the squatter's brains,
But Sandy had the stubborn blood
    Of Scotland in his veins;
He held the land and fenced it in,
    He cleared and ploughed the soil,
And year by year a richer crop
    Repaid him for his toil.

Between the homes for many years
    The devil left his tracks:
The squatter pounded Ross's stock,
    And Sandy pounded Black's.
A well upon the lower run
    Was filled with earth and logs,
And Black laid baits about the farm
    To poison Ross's dogs.

It was, indeed, a deadly feud
    Of class and creed and race,
But, yet, there was a Romeo
    And a Juliet in the case;
And more than once across the flats,
    Beneath the Southern Cross,
Young Robert Black was seen to ride
    With pretty Jenny Ross.

One Christmas time, when months of drought
    Had parched the western creeks,
The bush-fires started in the north
    And travelled south for weeks.
At night along the river-side
    The scene was grand and strange—
The hill-fires looked like lighted streets
    Of cities in the range.

The cattle-tracks between the trees
 Were like long dusky aisles,
And on a sudden breeze the fire
 Would sweep along for miles;
Like sounds of distant musketry
 It crackled through the brakes,
And o'er the flat of silver grass
 It hissed like angry snakes.

It leapt across the flowing streams
 And raced the pastures broad;
It climbed the trees, and lit the boughs,
 And through the scrubs it roared.
The bees fell stifled in the smoke
 Or perished in their hives,
And with the stock the kangaroos
 Went flying for their lives.

The sun had set on Christmas Eve,
 When, through the scrub-lands wide
Young Robert Black came riding home
 As only natives ride.
He galloped to the homestead door
 And gave the first alarm:
'The fire is past the granite spur,
 And close to Ross's farm.

'Now, father, send the men at once,
 They won't be wanted here;
Poor Ross's wheat is all he has
 To pull him through the year.'
'Then let it burn,' the squatter said;
 'I'd like to see it done—
I'd bless the fire if it would clear
 Selectors from the run.

'Go, if you will,' the squatter said,
 'You shall not take the men—
Go out and join your precious friends,

And don't come here again.'
'I won't come back,' young Robert cried,
    And, reckless in his ire,
He sharply turned his horse's head
    And galloped towards the fire.

And there for three long weary hours,
    Half-blind with smoke and heat,
Old Ross and Robert fought the flames
    That neared the ripened wheat,
The farmer's hand was nerved by fears
    Of danger and of loss;
And Robert fought the stubborn foe
    For the love of Jenny Ross.

But serpent-like the curves and lines
    Slipped past them, and between,
Until they reached the bound'ry where
    The old coach-road had been.
'The track is now our only hope,
    There we must stand,' cried Ross,
'For nought on earth can stop the fire
    If once it gets across.'

Then came a cruel gust of wind,
    And, with a fiendish rush,
The flames leapt o'er the narrow path
    And lit the fence of brush.
'The crop must burn!' the farmer cried,
    'We cannot save it now,'
And down upon the blackened ground
    He dashed the ragged bough.

But wildly, in a rush of hope,
    His heart began to beat,
For o'er the crackling fire he heard
    The sound of horses' feet
'Here's help at last,' young Robert cried,
    And even as he spoke

The squatter with a dozen men
    Came racing through the smoke.

Down on the ground the stockmen jumped
    And bared each brawny arm;
They tore green branches from the trees
    And fought for Ross's farm;
And when before the gallant band
    The beaten flames gave way,
Two grimy hands in friendship joined—
    And it was Christmas Day.

The Babies of Walloon

He was lengthsman on the railway, and his station scarce
    deserved
That 'pre-eminence in sorrow' of the Majesty he served,
But as dear to him and precious were the gifts reclaimed so
    soon—
Were the workman's little daughters who were buried near
    Walloon.

Speak their names in tones that linger, just as though you held
    them dear;
There are eyes to which the mention of those names will bring a
    tear.
Little Kate and Bridget, straying in an autumn afternoon,
Were attracted by the lilies in the water of Walloon.

All is dark to us. The angels sing perhaps in Paradise
Of the younger sister's danger, and the elder's sacrifice;
But the facts were hidden from us, when the soft light from the
    moon
Glistened on the water-lilies o'er the Babies at Walloon.

Ah! the children love the lilies, while we elders are inclined
To the flowers that have poison for the body and the mind.
Better for the 'strongly human' to have done with life as soon,
Better perish for a lily like the Babies of Walloon.

For they gather flowers early on the river far away,
Where the everlasting lilies keep their purity for aye,
And while summer brings our lilies to the run and the lagoon
May our children keep the legend of the Babies of Walloon.

Past Carin'

Now up and down the siding brown
    The great black crows are flyin',
And down below the spur, I know,
    Another 'milker's' dyin';
The crops have withered from the ground,
    The tank's clay bed is glarin',
But from my heart no tear nor sound,
    For I have gone past carin'—
        Past worryin' or carin',
        Past feelin' aught or carin';
        But from my heart no tear nor sound,
        For I have gone past carin'.

Through Death and Trouble, turn about,
    Through hopeless desolation,
Through flood and fever, fire and drought,
    And slavery and starvation;
Through childbirth, sickness, hurt, and blight,
    And nervousness an' scarin',
Through bein' left alone at night,
    I've got to be past carin',
        Past botherin' or carin'.
        Past feelin' and past carin';
        Through city cheats and neighbours' spite,
        I've come to be past carin'.

Our first child took, in days like these,
    A cruel week in dyin',
All day upon her father's knees,
    Or on my poor breast lyin';
The tears we shed—the prayers we said
    Were awful, wild—despairin'!

I've pulled three through, and buried two
    Since then—and I'm past carin'.
        I've grown to be past carin',
        Past worryin' and wearin';
        I've pulled three through and buried two
        Since then, and I'm past carin'.

'Twas ten years first, then came the worst,
    All for a barren clearin';
I thought, I thought my heart would burst
    When first my man went shearin';
He's drovin' in the great North-west,
    I don't know how he's farin';
For I, the one that loved him best,
    Have grown to be past carin'.
        I've grown to be past carin',
        Past waitin' and past wearin';
        The girl that waited long ago
        Has lived to be past carin'.

My eyes are dry, I cannot cry,
    I've got no heart for breakin',
But where it was in days gone by,
    A dull and empty achin'.
My last boy ran away from me,
    I know my temper's wearin',
But now I only wish to be
    Beyond all signs of carin'.
        Past wearyin' or carin',
        Past feelin' and despairin';
        And now I only wish to be
        Beyond all signs of carin'.

My Father-in-Law and I

My father-in-law is a careworn man,
    And a silent man is he;
But he summons a smile as well as he can
    Whenever he meets with me.

The sign we make with a silent shake
    That speaks of the days gone by—
Like men who meet at a funeral—
    My father-in-law and I.

My father-in-law is a sober man
    (And a virtuous man, I think);
But we spare a shilling whenever we can,
    And we both drop in for a drink.
Our pints they fill, and we say, 'Ah, well!'
    With the sound of the world-old sigh—
Like the drink that comes after a funeral—
    My father-in-law and I.

My father-in-law is a kindly man—
    A domestic man is he.
He tries to look cheerful as well as he can
    Whenever he meets with me.
But we stand and think till the second drink
    In a silence that might imply
That we'd both get over a funeral,
    My father-in-law and I.

Mary Fullerton
The Grain

All day along the hot headlands,
Old Darrant's scythe-blade swung;
A hundred times he wiped his brow,
And thrice his flannel wrung.

His daughter bent her aching back,
Fast flew her thorn-pricked hands
Tying the old man's reaping close
With its own golden bands.

The long swarths cut, the hard task done
She tossed the last sheaf bound;

'Hurrah!'—a ripple ran of Youth—
The grain showered on the ground.

He turned and struck her on the face,
'You'll waste my wheat again!'
Palely she fronted him, and mute—
'Twas HE that spilt the grain.

The Folk of Brenan's Lane

A child is sick down Brenan's Lane,
Where all the houses lean,
And many a roof lets in the rain
The broken slates between.

'Tis Salter's Tom who's fallen ill—
Got something in his bones;
The doctor named a long, long name—
As long as Tommy's groans.

All day a string of neighbors comes,
Sleeves up and hair run wild;
With just a cup of this or that
To tempt the poor sick child.

There's this one comes, and that one comes,
To do this job or that;
Or take the younger children off
From wrangling on the mat.

And not a night of all the month
But some intruding guest
Had made the tired mother go
And take a bit of rest.

Though food is scant and clothing mean,
And the roofs let in the rain,
I who have seen, declare there are
No poor in Brenan's Lane.

Christopher Brennan
From *The Wanderer*

I cry to you as I pass your windows in the dusk;

Ye have built you unmysterious homes and ways in the wood
where of old ye went with sudden eyes to the right and left;
and your going was now made safe and your staying comforted,
for the forest edge itself, holding old savagery
in unsearch'd glooms, was your houses' friendly barrier.
And now that the year goes winterward, ye thought to hide
behind your gleaming panes, and where the hearth sings merrily
make cheer with meat and wine, and sleep in the long night,
and the uncared wastes might be a crying unhappiness.
But I, who have come from the outer night, I say to you
the winds are up and terribly will they shake the dry wood:
the woods shall awake, hearing them, shall awake to be toss'd
    and riven,
and make a cry and a parting in your sleep all night
as the wither'd leaves go whirling all night along all ways.
And when ye come forth at dawn, uncomforted by sleep,
ye shall stand at amaze, beholding all the ways overhidden
with worthless drift of the dead and all your broken world:
and ye shall not know whence the winds have come, nor shall
    ye know
whither the yesterdays have fled, or if they were.

Mabel Forrest
The Cat in the Cupboard

There are plump lizards in the dusty grass,
And brown cockroaches that you might have had,
Green frogs that croak, and baby rats that hide
In bricked-in drains. Your fancy is instead
The caverns of a cupboard. Let one leave
A cupboard door ajar, and in you spring!

Bureau or press or anything that shuts!
Wardrobes where empty gowns hang rustling,
The soulless envelope of scented things.
Ever so softly let the handle turn,
And there you are with your white stockinged feet
As delicate as Agag's! In you step
Prying in every corner till at last
You settle down with an inquiring purr
To meet what Fate shall send!
Indeed I think
Your forbears have been reared in English homes,
In old ghost-haunted manors. And you hear
In memory still the little mouse that squeaks
In oaken wainscots, or in some clamped chest
Where grandmamma kept that bright Paisley shawl,
Or the white Cashmere that the Nabob sent,
With ribbons that were worn at Waterloo
By a slim officer with noisy spurs,
And great jackboots! I think the lavenders
Of sunken gardens cling about them still,
For cats love fragrant things that women store.
Belike your forbear from the Old World came—
A soldier's bride in snowy pantalettes,
And bonnet too severe for her small face.
(Who shuddered from her bridegroom's sheathed sword,
And dreamed at night of horrid visages
Scowling, where convicts huddled in the waist
Of the accursed ship!) An English girl,
With mittened hand and obvious wedding-ring,
Smuggled her pet from some grey parsonage
To meet the blaze of the Antipodes!
Or else a 'lifer's' sweetheart, following him
Over the blue of wide, adventurous seas
With tight plaid shawl held to her ample breast,
Brought your ancestor, clawing at the bag!
Maybe your great grandsires have met a king
Who had a queen at home, but knew a nest

35

Of dropping lilac-trees and hedges clipt
Inside stone walls that guard the secret well
Of that light lady from the provinces:
And your grandsire enjoyed a patch of sun,
And washed his ear and burnished up his tail,
And scorned the strutting peacock in his path;
Familiar with the merry ways of kings,
Watched the sword-stick, yet purred complacently,
Royal himself in poise, though presently
To drown his virtue in the pantry cream!
A tiger you become sometimes at dawn
In the wet grasses ambushing a bird.
On moonlit nights an emerald-eyed romance
You flit, a shadow into silences,
Leaving behind a gently swaying rose
You flicked in passing, till its censer spills
Musk on the tropic air, and still, I know
Your vice is cupboards—with the door ajar!

John Shaw Neilson
Marian's Child

First we thought of the river,
    But the body might be found;
And it did not seem so cruel
    To bury it in the ground.
So small it seemed, so helpless—
    I hardened my heart like stone—
She kissed it over and over,
    And then I heard her groan.

I took it out of her bosom:
    It cried, and cried, and cried;
I carried it down the garden—
    The moon was bright outside.
I dug a hold with a shovel
    And laid the baby down;

I shovelled the sand upon it—
  The sand was soft and brown.

But, ah! its cry was bitter—
  I scarce could cover it in,
And when at last 'twas hidden
  I sank beneath my sin.
Down at the foot of the garden,
  Where the moon-made shadows fell,
I sold myself to the Devil
  And bought a home in hell.

Down at the foot of the garden,
  Where the weeds grew rank and wild,
Under the shivering willows
  I murdered Marian's child;
My heart was wildly beating,
  My eyes and checks were wet,
For I heard the baby crying—
  O God! I hear it yet.
I hear it crying, crying,
  Just as I heard it cry
In Marian's arms in the morning
  When I knew that it must die.

*

Neither of us was woman—
  I was the younger one;
And we strove to tell each other
  What a wise thing we had done.
Why should it live to plague us?
  Why should it ever begin
Travelling roads of trouble,
  Soiling its soul with sin?

Marian! ah, she remembers!
  In spite of all her tears
Sweet children call her mother
  These many, many years.

Yet when I saw my darling,
    Her blue eyes seemed to swell:
'Annie!' she said, 'do you hear it?
    Listen! I hear it well!

'In the night I hear it calling
    With a muffled, plaintive wail,
And my heart stands still to sound its sobs,
    And always I try and fail;
For I think the depth of my baby's grief
    Will never fathomed be
Till the fires are lit in the bottomless pit
    To blast eternity.'

Once in a southern city
    Joy came into my life—
He loved me, kissed me, thought me
    Worthy to be his wife…
No, I will never marry.
    God! I had rather die—
If ever I had a baby
    'Twould curse me with its cry!
For down at the foot of the garden,
    Where the moon-made shadows fell,
I sold myself to the Devil
    And bought a home in hell.

Polly and Dad and the Spring Cart

The old man's putting Polly into the old Spring Cart
He bought it when he was married and I'll bet he thought it
    smart
He always counts on Polly as a first-rate trotting mare
In fact he reckons the whole turn-out quite a stylish affair.

The wheels are dished and the poor old cart is knocked about a
    lot
And Polly is old and lazy and lame and doesn't like to trot
We often tell the old man they're all on the track downhill

But his eyes flash up and he answers there's plenty of go in
    them still.

When the old man gets in liquor he's sure to get in a row
And the poor old chap it wouldn't take much to finish him
    right off now
So whenever he yokes up Polly and toddles into the town
Some of us go to fetch him out before the sun is down.

He usually goes to Riley's we always go there first
And when he's just a little bit on it's then we find him worst
We'd rather see him beastly drunk for then he's middling quiet
And we bundle him into the Spring cart and see if the tail-
    board's right.

Poor old man and poor old mare and poor old Spring cart too
Many a hundred miles they've gone when they were young and
    new
Many a mile they've gone in dust and many a mile in rain
But one of them some of these days will go and they'll never
    run again.

The old man often grumbles that his family all are gone
And most of them never seem to care a hang how he's getting
    on
And perhaps old Polly's motherly thoughts run in a similar way
For all her family too are gone except a black and a bay.

The first she had got killed in bolt and it's years and years ago
And a fine black filly was stolen running about Glencoe
And a handsome chestnut yearling that didn't have no brand
Was sold out of pound on the Sydney side and another died of
    sand.

And one we sold to a parson and the parson drives him hard
And one was swapped for a watch and chain to a cove at the
    Old Stock Yard
And a cocky owns another one still out Goulburn Valley way
And one belongs to a squatter down about Rivoli Bay.

And the old man's family likewise are scattered here and there
And dead is the mother who loved them and thought them very
    fair
She was proud of her girls and proud of her boys too
And worked and did for all of us all that a mother can do.

Watty went into the Army it keeps him from the drink
And Harry is in New Zealand he's mining there I think
And Nelly married a baker somewhere in South Aus.
And Lily is bar-maid in a pub over at Southern Cross.

And Fred is up in Queensland and he hasn't written for years
But we hear about him now and again from a station where he
    shears
And Tom is training horses and the last we heard of Bill
He was over in Tasmania working there at a mill.

And the only ones of the lot that are left are Jimmy and Belle
    and I
And I think it always our duty to keep a watchful eye
On poor old Dad and the poor old mare and the poor old
    Spring Cart too
Although he always reckons they're nearly as good as new.

The Vixen has Spoken

The Vixen has taken the lamb for its tongue
She said I am needing more milk for the young.

Full well I know famine and mother pain too
My heart shall not pity the heart of the ewe.

*

The women are mournful they meet and they pray
The long war has taken their treasures away.

They walk in the morning the dead lamb is there
How cruel is the vixen their voices declare.

*

The vixen has heard them, she holds a reply
These mothers are fiercer and redder than I.

These mothers do chide me a mother I am
And have not they eaten the heart of a lamb.

C. J. Dennis

From *The Songs of a Sentimental Bloke*

Uncle Jim

'I got no time fer wasters, lad,' sez 'e
   'Give me a man wiv grit,' sez Uncle Jim.
'E bores 'is cute old eyes right into me,
   While I stares 'ard an' gives it back to 'im.
Then orl at once 'e grips me 'and in 'is:
'Some'ow,' 'e sez, 'I likes yer ugly phiz.'

'You got a look,' 'e sez, 'like you could stay;
   Altho' yeh mauls King's English when yeh yaps,
An' 'angs flash frills on ev'rythink yeh say.
   I ain't no grammarist meself, per'aps,
But langwidge is a 'elp, I owns,' sez Unk,
'When things is goin' crook.' And 'ere 'e wunk.

'Yeh'll find it tough,' 'e sez, 'to knuckle down.
   Good farmin' is a gift—like spoutin' slang.
Yeh'll 'ave to cut the luxuries o' town,
   An' chuck the manners of this back-street gang;
Fer country life ain't cigarettes and beer.'
'I'm game,' I sez. Sez Uncle, 'Put it 'ere!'

Like that I took the plunge, an' slung the game.
   I've parted wiv them joys I 'eld most dear;
I've sent the leery bloke that bore me name
   Clean to the pack wivout one pearly tear;
An' frum the ashes of a ne'er-do-well
A bloomin' farmer's blossomin' like 'ell.

Farmer! That's me! Wiv this 'ere strong right 'and
    I've gripped the plough; and blistered jist a treat.
Doreen an' me 'as gone upon the land.
    Yours truly fer the burden an' the 'eat!
Yours truly fer upendin' chunks o' soil!
The 'ealthy, 'ardy, 'appy son o' toil!

I owns I've 'ankered fer me former joys;
    I've 'ad me hours o' broodin' on me woes;
I've missed the comp'ny, an' I've missed the noise,
    The football matches an' the picter shows.
I've missed—but, say, it makes me feel fair mean
To whip the cat; an' then see my Doreen.

To see the colour comin' in 'er cheeks,
    To see 'er eyes grow brighter day be day,
The new, glad way she looks an' laughs an' speaks
    Is worf ten times the things I've chucked away.
An' there's a secret, whispered in the dark,
'As made me 'eart sing like a flamin' lark.

Jist let me tell yeh 'ow it come about.
    The things that I've been thro' 'ud fill a book.
Right frum me birf Fate played to knock me out;
    The 'and that I 'ad dealt to me was crook!
Then comes Doreen, an' patches up me parst;
Now Forchin's come to bunk wiv me at larst.

First orf, one night poor Mar gits suddin fits,
    An' floats wivout the time to wave 'good-byes.'
Doreen is orl broke up the day she flits;
    It tears me 'eart in two the way she cries.
To see 'er grief, it almost made me glad
I never knowed the mar I must 'ave 'ad.

We done poor Muvver proud when she went out—
    A slap-up send-orf, trimmed wiv tears an' crape.
An' then fer weeks Doreen she mopes about,
    An' life takes on a gloomy sorter shape.

I watch 'er face git pale, 'er eyes grow dim;
Till—like some 'airy angel—comes ole Jim.

A cherub togged in sunburn an' a beard
    An' duds that shouted "Ayseed!" fer a mile:
Care took the count the minute 'e appeared,
    An' sorrer shrivelled up before 'is smile,
'E got the 'ammer-lock on my good-will
The minute that 'e sez, 'So, this is Bill.'

It's got me beat. Doreen's late Par, some way,
    Was second cousin to 'is bruvver's wife.
Somethin' like that. In less than 'arf a day
    It seemed 'e'd been my uncle orl me life.
'E takes me 'and: 'I dunno 'ow it is,'
'E sez, 'but, lad, I likes that ugly phiz.'

An' when 'e'd stayed wiv us a little while
    The 'ouse begun to look like 'ome once more.
Doreen she brightens up beneath 'is smile,
    An' 'ugs 'im till I kids I'm gettin' sore.
Then, late one night, 'e opens up 'is scheme,
An' passes me wot looks like some fond dream.

'E 'as a little fruit-farm, doin' well;
    'E saved a tidy bit to see 'im thro';
'E's gittin' old fer toil, an' wants a spell;
    An' 'ere's a 'ome jist waitin fer us two.
'It's 'er's an' yours fer keeps when I am gone,'
Sez Uncle Jim. 'Lad, will yeh take it on?'

So that's the strength of it. An' 'ere's me now
    A flamin' berry farmer, full o' toil;
Playin' joo-jitsoo wiv an 'orse an' plough,
    An' coaxin' fancy tucker frum the soil,
An' longin', while I wrestles with the rake,
Fer days when me poor back fergits to ache.

Me days an' nights is full of schemes an' plans
    To figger profits an' cut out the loss;

An' when the pickin's on, I 'ave me 'an's
    To take me orders while I act the boss;
It's sorter sweet to 'ave the right to rouse…
An' my Doreen's the lady of the 'ouse.

To see 'er bustlin' 'round about the place,
    Full of the simple joy of doin' things,
That thoughtful, 'appy look upon 'er face,
    That 'ope an' peace an' pride o' labour brings,
Is worth the crowd of joys I knoo one time,
An' makes regrettin' 'em seem like a crime.

An' ev'ry little while ole Uncle Jim
    Comes up to stay a bit an' pass a tip.
It gives us 'eart jist fer to look at 'im,
    An' feel the friendship in 'is warm 'and-grip.
'Im, wiv the sunburn on 'is kind old dile;
'Im, wiv the sunbeams in 'is sweet old smile.

'I got no time fer wasters, lad,' sez 'e,
    'But that there ugly mug o' yourn I trust.'
An' so I reckon that it's up to me
    To make a bloomin' do of it or bust.
I got to take the back-ache wiv the rest,
An' plug along, an' do me little best.

Luck ain't no steady visitor, I know;
    But now an' then it calls—fer look at me!
You wouldn't take me, 'bout a year ago,
    Free gratis wiv a shillin' pound o' tea;
Then, in a blessed 'eap, ole Forchin lands
A missus an' a farm fair in me 'ands.

Nina Murdoch

Socks

Two plain, purl two,
It's little else a woman can do
But bear sons and watch them grow,
Till marching out of her life they go.

44

Knit five, purl one,
I doubt if ever a mother's son
In war's cause hacked and cleft,
Knows half the hurt of the woman that's left.

Slip one, purl eight,
There's nothing left but to hope and wait,
And the seven tasks of Hercules
Would count as little compared with these.

Turn, slip, then the heel,
Out of sorrow comes haply weal,
But fair times are far away,
And there's many weep for their men to-day.

Cast off, the thing's done!
Many a husband and many a son
Find death in hapless war,
Nor ever know what they fought it for.

Two plain, purl two,
It's little else a woman can do
But bear sons and watch them grow,
Till marching out of her life they go.

Lesbia Harford
Fatherless

I've had no man
To guard and shelter me,
Guide and instruct me
From mine infancy.

No lord of earth
To show me day by day
What things a girl should do
And what she should say.

I have gone free
Of manly excellence

And hold their wisdom
More than half pretence.

For since no male
Has ruled me or has fed,
I think my own thoughts
In my woman's head.

The Wife

He's out of work!
I tell myself a change should mean a chance,
And he must look for changes to advance,
And he, of all men, really needs a jerk.

But I hate change.
I like my kitchen with its pans and pots
That shine like new although we've used them lots.
I wouldn't like a kitchen that was strange.

And it's not true
All changes are for better. Some are worse.
A man had rather work, though work's a curse,
Than mope at home with not a thing to do.

No surer thing
Than that he'll get another job. But soon!
Or else I'll have to change. This afternoon
Would be the time, before I sell my ring.

Elsie Cole

Fenella West

Fenella West is seventy-eight;
    She lives alone, alone;
The rosemary beside her gate
    Has tall and straggling grown.
Her husband and her sons are dead,
    Her girl across the sea

Dwells with the foreign man she wed,
   So all alone is she.

The waves die out in foamy signs
   A stone's throw from her wall;
Above her roof with eerie cries
   The wheeling seagulls call.
Her neighbours far to left and right
   In the sandy saltbush miles
Ask: 'Don't the winds blow shrill at night?'
   'Oh, yes,' she says; and smiles.

Fenella by the waters blue
   Finds driftwood for her fire;
She picks the little shells up, too,
   And loiters to admire
Their pink and fluted frailty,
   Their shining yellow wings.
'I've time to look at them,' says she,
   'The pretty, pretty things!'

So old, so queer, she must be mad.
   The neighbours shake their heads;
'That rosemary is dark and sad,
   But to your garden-beds
It brings back memories treasured well,
   You poor Fenella West?'
'Oh, yes,' she says, 'it's good to smell,
   But I like my roses best.'

She holds her mouth up to the sun,
   Throws kisses to the rain;
She greets the beauties one by one
   That wake each morn again.
'I've always wanted to stand still
   And watch awhile,' says she,
Drinking at last to deepest fill
   Leisure and privacy.

Fenella draws her curtain brown
    When sunset's glow is spent,
And by her bit of fire sits down
    And sighs for sheer content,
While from the driftwood's golden blaze
    Soft purple flamelets wreathe:
'I've lived for others all my days,
    But now I've time to breathe!'

Kenneth Slessor
From *Five Visions of Captain Cook*
V

After the candles had gone out, and those
Who listened had gone out, and a last wave
Of chimney-haloes caked their smoky rings
Like fish-scales on the ceiling, a Yellow Sea
Of swimming circles, the old man,
Old Captain-in-the-Corner, drank his rum
With friendly gestures to four chairs. They stood
Empty, still warm from haunches, with rubbed nails
And leather glazed, like agéd serving-men
Feeding a king's delight, the sticky, drugged
Sweet agony of habitual anecdotes.
But these, his chairs, could bear an old man's tongue,
Sleep when he slept, be flattering when he woke,
And wink to hear the same eternal name
From lips new-dipped in rum.

'Then Captain Cook,
I heard him, told them they could go
If so they chose, but he would get them back,
Dead or alive, he'd have them,'
The old man screeched, half-thinking to hear 'Cook!
Cook again! Cook! It's other cooks he'll need,
Cooks who can bake a dinner out of pence,

That's what he lives on, talks on, half-a-crown
A day, and sits there full of Cook.
Who'd do your cooking now, I'd like to ask,
If someone didn't grind her bones away?
But that's the truth, six children and half-a-crown
A day, and a man gone daft with Cook.'

That was his wife,
Elizabeth, a noble wife but brisk,
Who lived in a present full of kitchen-fumes
And had no past. He had not seen her
For seven years, being blind, and that of course
Was why he'd had to strike a deal with chairs,
Not knowing when those who chafed them had gone to sleep
Or stolen away. Darkness and empty chairs,
This was the port that Alexander Home
Had come to with his useless cutlass-wounds
And tales of Cook, and half-a-crown a day—
This was the creek he'd run his timbers to,
Where grateful countrymen repaid his wounds
At half-a-crown a day. Too good, too good,
This eloquent offering of birdcages
To gulls, and Greenwich Hospital to Cook,
Britannia's mission to the sea-fowl.

It was not blindness picked his flesh away,
Nor want of sight made penny-blank the eyes
Of Captain Home, but that he lived like this
In one place, and gazed elsewhere. His body moved
In Scotland, but his eyes were dazzle-full
Of skies and water farther round the world—
Air soaked with blue, so thick it dipped like snow
On spice-tree boughs, and water diamond-green,
Beaches wind-glittering with crumbs of gilt,
And birds more scarlet than a duchy's seal
That had come whistling long ago, and far
Away. His body had gone back,
Here it sat drinking rum in Berwickshire,

But not his eyes—they were left floating there
Half-round the earth, blinking at beaches milked
By suck-mouth tides, foaming with ropes of bubbles
And huge half-moons of surf. Thus it had been
When Cook was carried on a sailor's back,
Vengeance in a cocked hat, to claim his price,
A prince in barter for a longboat.
And then the trumpery springs of fate—a stone,
A musket-shot, a round of gunpowder,
And puzzled animals, killing they knew not what
Or why, but killing…the surge of goatish flanks
Armoured in feathers, like cruel birds:
Wild, childish faces, killing; a moment seen,
Marines with crimson coats and puffs of smoke
Toppling face-down; and a knife of English iron,
Forged aboard ship, that had been changed for pigs,
Given back to Cook between the shoulder-blades.
There he had dropped, and the old floundering sea,
The old, fumbling, witless lover-enemy,
Had taken his breath, last office of salt water.

Cook died. The body of Alexander Home
Flowed round the world and back again, with eyes
Marooned already, and came to English coasts,
The vague ancestral darknesses of home,
Seeing them faintly through a glass of gold,
Dim fog-shapes, ghosted like the ribs of trees
Against his blazing waters and blue air.
But soon they faded, and there was nothing left,
Only the sugar-cane and the wild granaries
Of sand, and palm-trees and the flying blood
Of cardinal-birds; and putting out one hand
Tremulously in the direction of the beach,
He felt a chair in Scotland. And sat down.

R. D. Fitzgerald

The Wind at Your Door

To Mary Gilmore

My ancestor was called on to go out—
a medical man, and one such must by law
wait in attendance on the pampered knout
and lend his countenance to what he saw,
lest the pet, patting with too bared a claw,
be judged a clumsy pussy. Bitter and hard,
see, as I see him, in that jailhouse yard.

Or see my thought of him: though time may keep
elsewhere tradition or a portrait still,
I would not feel under his cloak of sleep
if beard there or smooth chin, just to fulfil
some canon of precision. Good or ill
his blood's my own; and scratching in his grave
could find me more than I might wish to have.

Let him then be much of the middle style
of height and colouring; let his hair be dark
and his eyes green; and for that slit, the smile
that seemed inhuman, have it cruel and stark,
but grant it could be too the ironic mark
of all caught in the system—who the most,
the doctor or the flesh twined round that post?

There was a high wind blowing on that day;
for one who would not watch, but looked aside,
said that when twice he turned it blew his way
splashes of blood and strips of human hide
shaken out from the lashes that were plied
by one right-handed, one left-handed tough,
sweating at this paid task, and skilled enough.

That wind blows to your door down all these years.
Have you not known it when some breath you drew

tasted of blood? Your comfort is in arrears
of just thanks to a savagery tamed in you
only as subtler fears may serve in lieu
of thong and noose—old savagery which has built
your world and laws out of the lives it spilt.

For what was jailyard widens and takes in
my country. Fifty paces of stamped earth
stretch; and grey walls retreat and grow so thin
that towns show through and clearings—new raw birth
which burst from handcuffs—and free hands go forth
to win tomorrow's harvest from a vast
ploughland—the fifty paces of that past.

But see it through a window barred across,
from cells this side, facing the outer gate
which shuts on freedom, opens on its loss
in a flat wall. Look left now through the grate
at buildings like more walls, roofed with grey slate
or hollowed in the thickness of laid stone
each side the court where the crowd stands this noon.

One there with the officials, thick of build,
not stout, say burly (so this obstinate man
ghosts in the eyes) is he whom enemies killed
(as I was taught) because the monopolist clan
found him a grit in their smooth-turning plan,
too loyally active on behalf of Bligh.
So he got lost; and history passed him by.

But now he buttons his long coat against
the biting gusts, or as a gesture of mind,
habitual; as if to keep him fenced
from stabs of slander sticking him from behind,
sped by the schemers never far to find
in faction, where approval from one source
damns in another clubroom as of course.

This man had Hunter's confidence, King's praise;
and settlers on the starving Hawkesbury banks

recalled through twilight drifting across their days
the doctor's fee of little more than thanks
so often; and how sent by their squeezed ranks
he put their case in London. I find I lack
the hateful paint to daub him wholly black.

Perhaps my life replies to his too much
through veiling generations dropped between.
My weakness here, resentments there, may touch
old motives and explain them, till I lean
to the forgiveness I must hope may clean
my own shortcomings; since no man can live
in his own sight if it will not forgive.

Certainly I must own him whether or not
it be my will. I was made understand
this much when once, marking a freehold lot,
my papers suddenly told me it was land
granted to Martin Mason. I felt his hand
heavily on my shoulder, and knew what coil
binds life to life through bodies, and soul to soil.

There, over to one corner, a bony group
of prisoners waits; and each shall be in turn
tied by his own arms in a human loop
about the post, with his back bared to learn
the price of seeking freedom. So they earn
three hundred rippling stripes apiece, as set
by the law's mathematics against the debt.

These are the Irish batch of Castle Hill,
rebels and mutineers, my countrymen
twice over: first, because of those to till
my birthplace first, hack roads, raise roofs; and then
because their older land time and again
enrolls me through my forebears; and I claim
as origin that threshold whence we came.

One sufferer had my surname, and thereto
'Maurice', which added up to history once;

an ignorant dolt, no doubt, for all that crew
was tenantry. The breed of clod and dunce
makes patriots and true men: could I announce
that Maurice as my kin I say aloud
I'd take his irons as heraldry, and be proud.

Maurice is at the post. Its music lulls,
one hundred lashes done. If backbone shows
then play the tune on buttocks! But feel his pulse;
that's what a doctor's for; and if it goes
lamely, then dose it with these purging blows—
which have not made him moan; though, writhing there,
'Let my neck be,' he says, 'and flog me fair.'

One hundred lashes more, then rest the flail.
What says the doctor now? 'This dog won't yelp;
he'll tire you out before you'll see him fail;
here's strength to spare; go on!' Ay, pound to pulp;
yet when you've done he'll walk without your help,
and knock down guards who'd carry him being bid,
and sing no song of where the pikes are hid.

It would be well if I could find, removed
through generations back—who knows how far?—
more than a surname's thickness as a proved
bridge with that man's foundations. I need some star
of courage from his firmament, a bar
against surrenders: faith. All trials are less
than rain-blacked wind tells of that old distress.

Yet I can live with Mason. What is told
and what my heart knows of his heart, can sort
much truth from falsehood, much there that I hold
good clearly or good clouded by report;
and for things bad, ill grows where ills resort:
they were bad times. None know what in his place
they might have done. I've my own faults to face.

Mary Finnin
Mad Lucy

Mad Lucy who loved birds,
Pitied lost dogs,
Lived at the large end of the town
Where pavements run
To acres that realtors bit
But could not swallow—

But builders swallowed
Rod, pole and perch
While the boom lasted,
Leaving Lucy marooned
In the easement to the gully
Between a poultry farm
And the last lemon orchard.

And men with girls whose springing time
Took little note of calendar or care,
Emerging from the canyons of the city,
Rushed into matrimony and set up house,
Staking out a claim on permanence,
With thirty years to pay for their bush view
Daily diminishing to pale distance.

So a suburb is born
Of realtors' lust
And youth's folly.
But Lucy, bearded and serene,
Declares the sour gully
A bird sanctuary;
And come Fridays
Trundles a pram loaded
With love-bones for nobody's
Dogs.

The garden city
Teems with children
Born into the legend of Mad Lucy.
Their stones flailing upon the rusty shanty,
They lisp, 'Want Lulu, the mad ole girl!'
Their elders lift the summons to a chanty—
'We want Lulu, Lulu the fool!'

And one day when the inspector comes to school
With benevolent flourish giving the young dismissal,
(To talk of future citizens to their teachers).
They'll see a strangeness wispy in plain day—
They'll keep a witches' sabbath and fiesta;
They'll ring her cabin and when tired of play,
They'll hunt and trap her in the flowery gully,
Between the greenhoods and the cuckoo's cry—
The lover of loved birds and unloved dogs—
Mad Lucy.

A. D. Hope
Imperial Adam

Imperial Adam, naked in the dew,
Felt his brown flanks and found the rib was gone.
Puzzled he turned and saw where, two and two,
The mighty spoor of Jahweh marked the lawn.

Then he remembered through mysterious sleep
The surgeon fingers probing at the bone,
The voice so far away, so rich and deep:
'It is not good for him to live alone.'

Turning once more he found Man's counterpart
In tender parody breathing at his side.
He knew her at first sight, he knew by heart
Her allegory of sense unsatisfied.

The pawpaw drooped its golden breasts above
Less generous than the honey of her flesh;
The innocent sunlight showed the place of love;
The dew on its dark hairs winked crisp and fresh.

This plump gourd severed from his virile root,
She promised on the turf of Paradise
Delicious pulp of the forbidden fruit;
Sly as the snake she loosed her sinuous thighs,

And waking, smiled up at him from the grass;
Her breasts rose softly and he heard her sigh—
From all the beasts whose pleasant task it was
In Eden to increase and multiply

Adam had learned the jolly deed of kind:
He took her in his arms and there and then,
Like the clean beasts, embracing from behind,
Began in joy to found the breed of men.

Then from the spurt of seed within her broke
Her terrible and triumphant female cry,
Split upward by the sexual lightning stroke.
It was the beasts now who stood watching by:

The gravid elephant, the calving hind,
The breeding bitch, the she-ape big with young
Were the first gentle midwives of mankind;
The teeming lioness rasped her with her tongue;

The proud vicuña nuzzled her as she slept
Lax on the grass; and Adam watching too
Saw how her dumb breasts at their ripening wept,
The great pod of her belly swelled and grew,

And saw its water break, and saw, in fear,
Its quaking muscles in the act of birth,
Between her legs a pigmy face appear,
And the first murderer lay upon the earth.

On an Early Photograph of My Mother

Who would believe it to see her now, the mother
Of so many daughters and sons—and one of them I—
Dear busy old body, bustling around the sky
That this was indeed my darling, and no other?

Who would suppose to view her then, the tender
Bloom and dazzle of wildfire, and the stance
Of unripe grace, the naked eloquent glance,
Time could so tame or age despoil her splendour?

Or who imagine the imperceptible stages
From her madcap Then to this staid respectable Now?
One picture the Family Album does not show.
See where she ripped it angrily from the pages!

That is just the picture I should give most to recover,
When she changed to a molten mass and began to shrink
To a great smooth stone, and the stone began to think,
And she raged at her ruin and knew that her youth was over.

Did you destroy it, my darling, that face of granite
Cracked and scarred by your volcanic heart?
Did you take one look and tear it across and apart,
The barren body, the gaunt, unlovable planet?

You could not foresee this lovely old age beginning,
The ripeness, the breeding beauty. How could you know
Yourself with your lap full of flowers, soft-shouldered with
    snow,
Royally wearing your waters, your children pinning

Cities of lights at your breast, to show how clever they are?
Take comfort, my darling, and trundle your bulk through the
    sky:
Your cleverest children—and one of them is not I—
Are finding the trick that will turn you back to a star.

Cunning and cautious, but much less cautious than cunning,
They split small pieces of rock, a cup or two from your seas.

'Helping Mother!' they say, 'and busy as bees.
The noise we can make is tremendous; the flash is stunning.'

'We can do better,' they say. 'A surprise for Mother;
She will be pleased when we show her what we can do.'
How long will it take? Just another invention or two
And someone will press a button. You need not bother;

You will blaze out with the nimbus of youth, the limber
Liquid gait and the incandescent air;
You will forget the middle-aged ruin you were;
Good luck to you, darling! I shall not be there to remember.

Harry Hooton
Womb to Let

Oh where is my bonnie blue uniformed boy tonight—
    Coming in with one wing and a prayer?
God send him back safe to his mother's love
    After bombing christ out of every other's smother love
    Over there.
Oh my cuddly curly innocent god guide him safe to land—
    With the bloody stain of heaven's other urchin angels
    (Their noses no longer running now)
    On his baby hands.

Well why did you send him to war on others, moron mother?
    Couldn't you bear a man?
And why drag him back to the nest again—
    To re-enact in *his* sons the same foul plan?

But why did you have him at all?
    Was it because *you* were insufficient yourself,
Sex was insufficient in itself,
So that now you can't bear your boy, or any being
To be sufficient in himself?

Was it because you couldn't see love as something apart
    From reproduction and procreation—

As sheer production and creation,
   As the threshold of Art?

Or was it because, in common with all these other
   Mummies and Daddies,
You failed to make anything more significant of your own lives
   Than husbands and wives—
   Bore babies to sink or swim;
And visited your vile terms of family frustration—
   Your motherland, fatherland, bother and loverland,
   God up above land,
   Goodies and Baddies,
On the next generation—
   Left your fight for a new world to him?

Ronald McCuaig
Au Tombeau de Mon Père

1 went on Friday afternoons
Among the knives and forks and spoons
Where mounted grindstones flanked the floor
To my father's office door.

So serious a man was he,
The Buyer for the Cutlery…
I found him sketching lamps from stock
In his big stock-records book,

And when he turned the page to me:
'Not bad for an old codger, eh?'
I thought this frivolous in him,
Preferring what he said to them:

They wanted reparations paid
In German gold and not in trade,
But he rebuked such attitudes:
'You'll have to take it out in goods.'

And what they did in time was just,
He said, what he had said they must:

If Time had any end in sight
It was, to prove my father right.

The evening came, and changed him coats,
Produced a rag and rubbed his boots,
And then a mirror and a brush
And smoothed his beard and his moustache;

A sign for blinds outside to fall
On shelves and showcases, and all
Their hammers, chisels, planes and spades,
And pocket-knives with seven blades.

Then, in the lift, the patted back:
'He's growing like you, Mr Mac!'
(The hearty voices thus implied
A reason for our mutual pride.)

And so the front-door roundabout
Gathered us in and swept us out
To sausage, tea in separate pots,
And jellies crowned with creamy clots.

And once he took me on to a
Recital, to hear Seidel play,
And Hutchens spanked the piano-bass,
Never looking where it was.

When I got home I practised this,
But somehow always seemed to miss,
And my cigar-box violin,
After Seidel's, sounded thin.

And once he took me to a bill
Of sporadic vaudeville.
A man and woman held the stage;
She sneered in simulated rage,

And when he made a shrewd reply
He'd lift his oval shirt-front high
And slap his bare and hairy chest
To celebrate his raucous jest.

Then, as the shout of joy ensued,
Uniting mime and multitude,
And mine rang out an octave higher,
A boy-soprano's in that choir,

My father's smile was half unease,
Half pleasure in his power to please:
'Try not to laugh so loudly, Ron;
Those women think you're catching on.'

But far more often it was to
The School of Arts we used to go;
Up the dusty stairway's gloom,
Through the musty reading-room

And out to a veranda-seat
Overlooking Hunter Street.
There in the dark my father sat,
Pipe in mouth, to meditate.

A cake-shop glowed across the way
With a rainbow-cake display;
I never saw its keeper there,
And never saw a customer,

And yet there was activity
High in the south-western sky:
A bottle flashing on a sign
Advertising someone's wine.

So, as my father thought and thought
(Considering lines of saws he'd bought,
Or, silence both his church and club,
Feeling close to Nature's hub,

Or maybe merely practising
Never saying anything,
Since he could go, when deeply stirred,
Months, at home, without a word,

Or pondering the indignity
Of having to put up with me),

I contemplated, half awake,
The flashing wine, the glowing cake:

The wine that no one can decant,
And the cake we didn't want:
As Mr Blake's Redeemer said,
'This the wine, and this the bread.'

Elizabeth Riddell
News of a Baby

Welcome, baby, to the world of swords
And deadlier words.
We offer you a rough bed, and tears at morning,
And soon a playground
Bounded by ice and stones,
A buttonhole of thorns,
A kiss on war's corner.

We promise you, baby,
The stumble of fear in the heart,
The lurch of fear in the bones.

Painted upon your mother's cheek already
I see the dark effusion of your blood,
Bending already beside her patient chair the bandaged ghosts.
Welcome, baby, no dread thing will be omitted.
We are your eager hosts.

The Other Face

What she most fears
and looks for is the chiding mouth,
flirtatious lock of hair,
the blue glance avoiding hers.
She fears to see identical in the glass
the vain and challenging look,
her mother's look.

She has trivial memories of her,
pretty in pretty clothes,
resisting relegation to the widow's role.
There was distance between them.
They did not speak much,
using oblique stares across the silence.

She remembers being told to keep her elbows in
when eating, and to open doors for aunts.
She does not remember being warned against liars
or the penalties of dishonour and certainly not of evil.
If no evil, how could she learn of good?

There would be a man somewhere in a photo,
just to the right, a step behind
the woman in a hat and fur, with henna'd hair.

She feels guilty now, herself having learned
how cold the heart can be. She should have touched,
at least have said goodbye.

Now she fears to look in the mirror and see
the face behind her face.

Suburban Evening

This is the picture I have of you:
such a pretty woman and so melancholy
saying goodbye to your son in the leafy evening street
as if he were going to Gallipoli or the moon
or he might be going to depose the Soga clan
or to join Sobieski against the Turks at Lamberg.

His arm is around your shoulder which seems suddenly
to have grown tender, confiding, sad.

We had been listening to Adelina Patti on record
singing from *La Sonnambula*. She was sixty-three then
as you are now. She was the queen of song
and terror of entrepreneurs.

In the house there was the glint of metal
from your son's sabre, or his shield. And a great dog
strode softly beside you.

Your husband walked with a guest
making small talk (the economy, traffic, gardening)
and your daughter-in-law silently,
stepping angled because of the jutting baby
which seems to have an arrogant gait of its own,
brings up the rear.

In the street the starlings adjust their wings
preparing for the crash of artillery and for bombs to fall.
It is nothing, really, there is no adventure, nor war.
He is going home to another suburb
where his garden sleeps awaiting the spade,
and taking his wife and his dog and the unborn child.

Barbara Giles
Dans le Jardin de Mon Père, les Lilas ont Fleuri

Not in my father's garden,
three tied staked bundles of perennial phlox
bordered by bleeding heart and london pride
sole blossoming each year
lawns barbered daisies poisoned
three tall poplars trees from a child's ark.

One for you and one for me
and one for baby bunting.

Father worked hard and soon he was manager
the children at school did not speak like my father
we took a house down at rosebud each christmas holidays
mother bought the wrong clothes she made small economies
we had our own eggs she ran up our uniforms
only the teachers approved us reservedly.

Hickety, pickety my black hen
laying eggs for not quite gentlemen.

The people next door despised us they kept servants
dark trees faded their grass flowers ran wild
the children of her amplitude needed no correction
though we lacked savoir faire we were useful companions
and father subdued the mad murderous housemaid
the coat ripped from his back
the one time he set foot in the house.

Dinners for master cocktails for dame
no room for the people down the lane.

A life is too short to forget a childhood
the illspun strands cannot be plucked from the web
though flowers spill over the grass gowns have the right labels
the pictures on my walls are all good originals
I speak very nicely I have letters after my name
and the books on my shelves fall like flowers to the floor

Here am I little jumping joan
nobody's with me I'm always alone.

Infidel

Disloyal feet, quick-stepping,
here in the summer city.
Sunlight dapples the alleys.
I am here on hard business
as widow, signing myself
into a new way of life.

But the air is champagne and shop windows
are chockful of fripperies. Women
have never looked better,
the season's mode admirable.

A fine whiff of coffee
teases the nostrils. This heavy
business of dying should slow me
but the body is living and traitorous.

Mama's Little Girl

An unlucky year
in a strange city
with a crazed husband
when you, my little girl,
said you were coming.

The house looked respectable.
In another room
someone was playing Mozart.
'Just grit your teeth.' And after
I walked soft-legged out,
having put off your visit
permanently, little one.

With better times, tall sons.

In iron-hard necessity I left you
upon the mountain for the bears to take.
A kind of logic says she was our daughter.

Vera Newsom

Sligo

Children. I have sowed them to the wind
to call in their own voices, my themes like trees
snapped in the storm.

The river hurtles over the weir,
swerves under Sligo bridge. I feel
the electric shock when molecule

hits molecule, beating the spume to a froth.
A white bird flaps its wings,
rises above the stream, lifts high

beyond the roof tops, hiding itself in cloud
where the stone houses stride along the ridge.
Those roofs of neatly patterned slate,

this horizontal curve of the river wall
define a mind's geometry. Even the weir
which makes such agitation in the stream

rebutting the water's weight…How I play
with thought, like a child with coloured glass,
let it drop, shattering the natural images;

then, careless if the fingers bleed, stoop down
to pick the splinters up. Children,
those dark currents of the blood,

children's children scatter their spray
like crystal in the light of the sun,
fall back, submerged. But for me

those years of poetry I did not write
are lost in that deep stream.

My Grandmother Singing

Rain falls on the fine grass,
its minute blades
like knives at the throat.
Birds with their chatter
interstitch the rain—

Like my grandmother's treble,
high-pitched, double-stopping,
a fiddle's split note.

And the cruel blades of the grass
gleam in the wet light,
saw at the frayed string.

The voice quavers, hesitates,
the knife edges her throat
and the stretched cords splinter…

But still that high-pitched treble
intersperses the birds' din
and the small rain pierces
the thin blades of grass.

John Blight
Houses and Homes

Houses and homes were important in my
youth. Now I am at home in the wilderness—
by which I mean, not the bush or the city,
but among the bewildered.

Homes are where
my mother resided. The houses—later
domicile? She lives in my memory
and I am at home. The big houses—the
big homes? My father liked rooms about him.

My mother was a cottager at heart…
and I? I have lived in the heart and found
that place warm and cold by degrees as graded
as the front and back stairs. Most of our
residences were of timber, on stumps; but
that last big house had to be brick, I
believe, because brick smothers sounds and
parents can argue beyond the family's hearing.

Not understanding a heart's breakages
(my own, intact, beat off the clutch of death)
I learnt that hearts break up in marriages;
though my two parents were never divorced.

Both held their pride of which I was not proud,
but am glad to remember now. There were
no losers, no brutalities—but words…and
how separate are their meanings!

                                        I play
          with words here, again to remind you, there is
          distinction between a house and a home.

                        Family Ties

          Don't knock family ties—they knot
          on the winds of altercations,
          peculiarly untangle
          with smiles, tiffs ironed out without
          a board of dispute. Sometimes I
          believe they are all heart, bury
          the smart replies of the mind,
          seal up tunnels of escape to
          vituperations. Just as well
          the flesh takes hold of them, lets the
          mind down pits where brains may never
          cogitate upon a final
          rejoinder. There must be some mute
          share of soul in the family.

              # Flexmore Hudson
              Giovanni Rinaldo, P.O.W.

He had heard in a wind cooling his wounds of fire,
in the whisper of the mango to the moon that climbed the wire,

Maria, his wife, and Nino, the son of their tears,
calling more sweetly than Death, all through the years.

Nearer now and surer they sound, so he ploughs
the frosty fallow singing and, fetching our cows

home through the yaccas that burn on the misty flats,
he sings as the sundown dislodges the owls and the bats.

At school my youngster Billy boasts of the size
of the stones by our swamp that his friend the prisoner shies,

so Giovanni is coaxed into feats of strength and tussles
by little boys brought home to admire his bulging muscles.

And my wife and daughters go humming unawares,
I, too, the saddest of Sicilian airs.

Last night his laughter surrendered the outposts of pride,
and, moaning, he rushed from the table to his room outside;

and the crumpled paper told us our troops were bombarding
the town his sleepless prayers had long been guarding.

'Dio buono!' he moaned—and his wife's name—
sending his heart to an orchard dissolved in flame;

while the little photos he had often shown us streamed
blood down our minds as we listened, and then as we dreamed.

Cutting chaff this morning, I heard the birds,
the sheep, and the engine itself, dinning the words,
'Dio buono!'

And they told me that Billy, staring wide-eyed
while the rest of the class were writing, suddenly sighed,
'Dio buono!'

Joyce Lee
My Father's Country

I can close my eyes one heartbeat
and smell the Wimmera summers of the twenties,
call up cloud continents
through incredible blue gateways,
breaking stubbled plains on Grampians rock.

This is my father's country. Manager of the flour mill
he belongs in a crowded picture. His friends
are busy, flour-dusted ghosts
lumping wheat from Rainbow, Patchewollock, Brim.

Even on Sundays he spars with a string of stationmasters,
pleading for trucks to feed Manila, Mauritius, Hong Kong.

Upstaging him, especially on Sundays, is George Freeman
polishing his darling the steam engine,
lighting her fires with Mallee wood. A new mill
four storey brick and diesel
retires him from the corrugated iron shed
too soon. He spends the extra time
popping his red bright face over the fence to chat with anyone.

At first light, I can smell hot dust from wagons creaking past
my sleepout. In slow procession to the weighbridge,
each farmer, bolstered by a sewnup harvest, gentles
six outsize horses with a flick
of sunblackened hands. An old felt hat
scalloped by seasons of sweaty tides, crowns the load.

Eventually, I find my engine under a mountain
where timbercutters left her
the last day. Saplings dance on the dappled body
buried to the knees in wildflowers. Far
from my father's niche at the Necropolis,
George Freeman lies, cellar cool in Wimmera clay.
Safe from death, I keep them in endless summer.

Kenneth Mackenzie
A Fairy Tale
FOR ELIZABETH

Why should you wake, my darling, at this hour,
in this unhaunted nurse-room of your sleep?
The street is silent, echoing your screams
with shocked politeness; the clock ticks past four—
it is no time for dreams.
Only a vanishing trail of footsteps keeps
smartly in time with time. Come—turn over,

hide your twisted face under the blue cover,
and cover your bared soul with shaking hands:
It is too naked, and we are alone,
and I am not young enough to understand,
only to pity your trembling stare,
your hopeless moaning.
Terror has struck me, too; it is older than age,
old as the simple cell, old as air,
helplessly aware of doom—
the last page turning—
but why in the fastidious silence of this room?

Am I to believe, in spite of night,
sleep, solitude, security, warmth, love
all nursing you, your mind, remembering,
heard the sound of engines in flight?
Through the dark skin of sleep did come
the roar of the drumskin, and the whistling?
The drum—did you hear the drum?
Maybe, then, with the whole world turned to metal
you watched through shut eyes on the eyelids' screen
the abattoirs in action, much death
of howling flesh, but not the flesh of cattle.
Between the taking and the relinquishment of a breath
all that will be, is, must have been,
backwards and forwards on the screen runs
in chaos, generating terror, griping
the tangle of bowels—the fighting on the dunes,
slaughter among mountains, under suns
torrid and dusty, in snows, in the dark,
in the dawn and at twilight. Death sniping
merrily from the void wipes out a city,
and with a mighty shout as of one voice
we all scream 'Pity—give pity! And money!' and then
are seen, in the exploding crash and roar
of chambered flame released, to be men
(or women) impressed by so much devastation:

The like of it has never been seen before,
and it's the proof of our age, civilization—
You see it in a bombshell in the night,
and you, my darling, suck it out of the air
into your sleep, and dream it really is true.
No! this is a fairy story for small girls,
a tale so well-devised, so rare,
it even convinced you!
Wait till to-morrow's imperial dawn unfolds
its east red-white-blue banner, you will see
nothing so evil under such a flag could be.

Turn and sleep again.
The sound you dreamed was just our old friend thunder
roaring with pain.
The wet and splashing torrents, that showed red
through eyelids closed on open dreaming eyes,
were only rain,
and the footsteps have walked up into the sky,
away at the street's end. In this bed
is nothing but a small warm girl who must
always, always sleep very peacefully
and not scream in the night—

                                    (I trust. I trust.)

Dorothy Auchterlonie
Equation

*'If a man were to give all the substance of his
house for love, it would utterly be contemned'*

The sum came out quite neatly. According to the rules.
He put his pen down, sighed with relief.
Much easier than he'd thought.
Went home early to dinner, was rewarded with a kiss.
Lunched at the club next day,
And spoke vigorously at the monthly meeting.
As he went on his rounds, or dug the garden,

His public image smiled back once more
At its inventors.
Everything was normal again. As far as he knew.
And if a public image makes a cold bed-fellow,
Well, people have to choose in this life.
              Not long after, he set out for the next.
Took the sum with him, just for the record.
—It's all right, I think, he said modestly,
I checked the figures twice:
Profession, children, colleagues, wife,
Customers, relations, friends,
They're all there...
—Are they? said God mildly, running his finger down the page.
You remind me of a young man I knew once in Galilee.
Nice chap. Too much money, though...His finger paused.
—There's a symbol missing, said God gently.
You've left it out. In my algebra
Everything has to be taken into account . . .
—Missing? he said, and shifted his weight to the other foot.
—The woman I gave you, said God. So that you
   might know who you are.
Not the habit you lived with, acquired in accordance with
   custom.
But the woman I gave you, said God. Did you not notice my
   seal?
What happened to her?
He took his celestial pen and altered a number.
—The answer, said God,
Should be nought.
There was silence in Heaven
For about half an hour.
—Where is she? he whispered, from behind his hands.
—Oh, she's here, said God. Came some time ago.
You can see her if you like, said God.
From a distance, He added, walking away.
But you will never be able to touch her.
Never.

David Campbell
Town Planning

The plover cries in air
For the town has grown
And hatched its brick cottages
Amongst the stone.

Where young lambs danced
By grave-faced sheep,
Five hundred pretty housewives
Wake and sleep.

Nine months later,
And not one day more,
There's a new baby-carriage
By each front door.

Five hundred children
And the nappies to dry—
The housewives gossip,
Grow old and die.

Overhead the plover,
Like the moon apart,
Tells his lonely knowledge
Of the human heart.

Mothers and Daughters

The cruel girls we loved
Are over forty,
Their subtle daughters
Have stolen their beauty;

And with a blue stare
Of cool surprise,
They mock their anxious mothers
With their mothers' eyes.

The Australian Dream

The doorbell buzzed. It was past three o'clock.
The steeple-of-Saint-Andrew's weathercock
Cried silently to darkness, and my head
Was bronze with claret as I rolled from bed
To ricochet from furniture. Light! Light
Blinded the stairs, the hatstand sprang upright,
I fumbled with the lock, and on the porch
Stood the Royal Family with a wavering torch.

'We hope,' the Queen said, 'we do not intrude.
The pubs were full, most of our subjects rude.
We came before our time. It seems the Queen's
Command brings only, "Tell the dead marines!"
We've come to you.' I must admit I'd half
Expected just this visit. With a laugh
That put them at their ease, I bowed my head.
'Your Majesty is most welcome here,' I said.
'My home is yours. There is a little bed
Downstairs, a boiler-room, might suit the Duke.'
He thanked me gravely for it and he took
Himself off with a wave. 'Then the Queen Mother?
She'd best bed down with you. There is no other
But my wide bed. I'll curl up in a chair.'
The Queen looked thoughtful. She brushed out her hair
And folded up *The Garter* on a pouf.
'Distress was the first commoner, and as proof
That queens bow to the times,' she said, 'we three
Shall share the double bed. Please follow me.'
I waited for the ladies to undress—
A sense of fitness, even in distress,
Is always with me. They had tucked away
Their state robes in the lowboy; gold crowns lay
Upon the bedside tables; ropes of pearls
Lassoed the plastic lampshade; their soft curls
Were spread out on the pillows and they smiled.
'Hop in,' said the Queen Mother. In I piled

Between them to lie like a stick of wood.
I couldn't find a thing to say. My blood
Beat, but like rollers at the ebb of tide.
'I hope your Majesties sleep well,' I lied.
A hand touched mine and the Queen said, 'I am
Most grateful to you, Jock. Please call me Ma'am.'

From *Starting from Central Station*
Angina

He feared angina from his thirtieth year:
A doctor, he knew what to fear.
On the stair I saw him stop,
Take his pulse and climb the mountain top.

Drought, boredom, loneliness, could bring it on,
And his unlikely son:
Deeper than Eros' dart
Care struck my father's heart.

On Kismet, his roan mare,
He cut out cow and steer;
Then chained up his blue heeler, and
For fear of germs, scrubbed hand on hand.

1 do the same myself now. But in Scot
He said at our last row, 'You'll nae forget,'
And climbed to fix a mill. At seventy-three
Was it angina or did he die of me?

Michael Thwaites
Coming into the Clyde

Part of me for ever is the January morning
Coming into the Clyde in the frosty moonlight
And the land under snow and the snow under moonlight,
Fall upon fall, a soundless ecstasy.

I alone on the bridge, below me the helmsman
Whistling softly to the listening voicepipe,
And no sound else but the washing of the bow-wave
As the buoys go by like marching pylons.

I gaze from the glory of the bared universe
To the guarded secret of the winter world
Rapt, and the helmsman now is silent,
And I wait for the time to alter course.

To port lift the magic scenario mountains
White above the shoulders of Holy Island,
And nearer, clear as a square-lined coverlet,
All the fields and hedges on the slopes of Arran.

But further and smaller, away to starboard,
The plaited hills of Ayrshire gleam,
And I in thought am over them all
Away to my darling and my little son.

Beyond the moonlit hills that morning
My darling lay, and my little son;
But she in her cold bed lone and waking,
And he in the frozen ground asleep.

Judith Wright
Two Dreamtimes
FOR KATH WALKER

Kathy my sister with the torn heart,
I don't know how to thank you
for your dreamtime stories of joy and grief
written on paperbark.

You were one of the dark children
I wasn't allowed to play with—
riverbank campers, the wrong colour,
(I couldn't turn you white).

So it was late I met you,
late I began to know
they hadn't told me the land I loved
was taken out of your hands.

Sitting all night at my kitchen table
with a cry and a song in your voice,
your eyes were full of the dying children,
the blank-eyed taken women,

the sullen looks of the men who sold them
for rum to forget the selling,
the hard rational white faces
with eyes that forget the past.

With a knifeblade flash in your black eyes
that always long to be blacker,
your Spanish-Koori face
of a fighter and singer,

arms over your breast folding
your sorrow in to hold it,
you brought me to you some of the way
and came the rest to meet me,

over the desert of red sand
came from your lost country
to where I stand with all my fathers,
their guilt and righteousness.

Over the rum your voice sang
the tales of an old people,
their dreaming buried, the place forgotten...
We too have lost our dreaming.

We the robbers robbed in turn,
selling this land on hire-purchase;
what's stolen once is stolen again
even before we know it.

If we are sisters, it's in this—
our grief for a lost country,

the place we dreamed in long ago,
poisoned now and crumbling.

Let us go back to that far time,
I riding the cleared hills,
plucking blue leaves for their eucalypt scent,
hearing the call of the plover,

in a land I thought was mine for life.
I mourn it as you mourn
the ripped length of the island beaches,
the drained paperbark swamps.

The easy Eden-dreamtime then
in a country of birds and trees
made me your shadow-sister, child,
dark girl I couldn't play with.

But we are grown to a changed world:
over the drinks at night
we can exchange our separate griefs,
but yours and mine are different.

A knife's between us. My righteous kin
still have cruel faces.
Neither you nor I can win them,
though we meet in secret kindness.

I am born of the conquerors,
you of the persecuted.
Raped by rum and an alien law,
progress and economics,

are you and I and a once-loved land
peopled by tribes and trees;
doomed by traders and stock exchanges,
bought by faceless strangers.

And you and I are bought and sold,
our songs and stories too
though quoted low in a falling market
(publishers shake their heads at poets).

Time that we shared for a little while,
telling sad tales of women
(black or white at a different price)
meant much and little to us.

My shadow-sister, I sing to you
from my place with my righteous kin,
to where you stand with the Koori dead,
'Trust none—not even poets.'

The knife's between us. I turn it round,
the handle to your side,
the weapon made from your country's bones.
I have no right to take it.

But both of us die as our dreamtime dies.
I don't know what to give you
for your gay stories, your sad eyes,
but that, and a poem, sister.

For a Pastoral Family
I   To My Brothers

Over the years, horses have changed to land-rovers.
Grown old, you travel your thousands of acres
deploring change and the wickedness of cities
and the cities' politics; hoping to pass to your sons
a kind of life you inherited in your generation.
Some actions of those you vote for stick in your throats.
There are corruptions one cannot quite endorse;
but if they are in our interests, then of course...

Well, there are luxuries still,
including pastoral silence, miles of slope and hill,
the cautious politeness of bankers. These are owed
to the forerunners, men and women
who took over as if by right a century and a half
in an ancient difficult bush. And after all
the previous owners put up little fight,
did not believe in ownership, and so were scarcely human.

Our people who gnawed at the fringe
of the edible leaf of this country
left you a margin of action, a rural security,
and left to me
what serves as a base for poetry,
a doubtful song that has a dying fall.

II To My Generation

A certain consensus of echo, a sanctioning sound,
supported our childhood lives. We stepped
on sure and conceded ground.
A whole society
extended a comforting cover of legality.
The really deplorable deeds
had happened out of our sight, allowing us innocence.
We were not born, or there was silence kept.

If now there are landslides, if our field of reference
is much eroded, our hands show little blood.
We enter a plea: Not Guilty.
For the good of the Old Country,
the land was taken; the Empire had loyal service.
Would any convict us?
Our plea has been endorsed by every appropriate jury.

If my poetic style, your pastoral produce,
are challenged by shifts in the market
or a change of taste, at least we can go down smiling
with enough left in our pockets
to be noted in literary or local histories.

III For Today

We were always part of a process. It has expanded.
What swells over us now is a logical spread
from the small horizons we made—
the heave of the great corporations

whose bellies are never full.
What sort of takeover bid
could you knock back now if the miners,
the junk-food firms or their processors want your land?
Or worse, leave you alone to hoe
small beans in a dwindling row?

The fears of our great-grandfathers—
apart from a fall in the English market—
were of spearwood, stone axes. Sleeping
they sprang awake at the crack
of frost on the roof, the yawn and stretching
of a slab wall. We turn on the radio
for news from the U.S.A. and U.S.S.R.
against which no comfort or hope
might come from the cattle prizes at the Show.

IV   Pastoral Lives

Yet a marginal sort of grace
as I remember it, softened our arrogant clan.
We were fairly kind to horses
and to people not too different from ourselves.
Kipling and A. A. Milne were our favourite authors
but Shelley, Tennyson, Shakespeare stood on our shelves—
suitable reading for women,
to whom, after all, the amenities had to be left.

An undiscursive lot (discourse is for the city)
one of us helped to found a university.
We respected wit in others,
though we kept our own for weddings,
unsure of the bona fides of the witty.

In England, we called on relatives,
assuming welcome for the sake of a shared bloodline,
but kept our independence.
We would entertain them equally, if they came

and with equal hospitality—
blood being thicker than thousands of miles of waters—
for the sake of Great-aunt Charlotte and old letters.

At church, the truncate, inarticulate
Anglican half-confession
'there is no health in us'
made us gag a little. We knew we had no betters
though too many were worse.
We passed on the collection-plate
adding a reasonable donation.

That God approved us was obvious.
Most of our ventures were prosperous.
As for the *Dies Irae*
we would deal with that when we came to it.

V   Change

At best, the men of our clan
have been, or might have been,
like Yeats' fisherman.
A small stream, narrow but clean,

running apart from the world.
Those hills might keep them so,
granite, gentle and cold.
But hills erode, streams go

through settlement and town
darkened by chemical silt.
Dams hold and slow them down,
'trade thickens them like guilt.

All men grow evil with trade
as all roads lead to the city.
Willie Yeats would have said,
perhaps, the more the pity.

But how can we be sure?
Wasn't his chosen man
as ignorant as pure?
Keep out? Stay clean? Who can?

VI   Kinship

Blue early mist in the valley. Apricots
bowing the orchard trees, flushed red with summer,
loading bronze-plaqued branches;
our teeth in those sweet buttock-curves. Remember
the horses swinging to the yards, the smell
of cattle, sweat and saddle-leather?
Blue ranges underlined the sky. In any weather
it was well, being young and simple,
letting the horses canter home together.

All those sights, smells and sounds we shared
trailing behind grey sheep, red cattle,
from Two-rail or Ponds Creek
through tawny pastures breathing pennyroyal.
In winter, sleety winds bit hands and locked
fingers round reins. In spring, the wattle.

With so much past in common,
on the whole we forgive each other
for the ways in which we differ—
two old men, one older woman.
When one of us falls ill,
the others may think less
of today's person, the lined and guarding face,

than of a barefoot child running careless through
long grass where snakes lie, or forgetting
to watch in the paddocks for the black Jersey bull.
Divisions and gulfs deepen
daily, the world over

more dangerously than now between us three.
Which is why, while there is time (though not our form at all)
I put the memories into poetry.

Jack Davis
The First-born

Where are my first-born, said the brown land, sighing;
They came out of my womb long, long ago.
They were formed of my dust—why, why are they crying
And the light of their being barely aglow?

I strain my ears for the sound of their laughter.
Where are the laws and the legends I gave?
Tell me what happened, you whom I bore after.
Now only their spirits dwell in the caves.

You are silent, you cringe from replying.
A question is there, like a blow on the face.
The answer is there when I look at the dying,
At the death and neglect of my dark proud race.

Dingo

What can I do for you dingo now?
There's still a price on your head.
The stockmen curse and swear and say
They want you scalped and dead.

You and my people roamed this land
Thousands of years before
The booted foot and the cloven hoof
Came from another shore.

Yes, they killed my people too
Before the yoke was set.
So run, my dingo brother, run:
We'll win our battle yet.

James McAuley
Pietà

A year ago you came
Early into the light.
You lived a day and night,
Then died; no-one to blame.

Once only, with one hand,
Your mother in farewell
Touched you. I cannot tell,
I cannot understand

A thing so dark and deep,
So physical a loss:
One touch, and that was all

She had of you to keep.
Clean wounds, but terrible,
Are those made with the Cross.

Numbers and Makes

The house we lived in faced the western line.
I used to sit and write the number down
Of every locomotive as it passed:
From the humdrum all-stations-into-town,

To the great thunderers that shook the house.
And passengers would wave back from the train.
I would watch out for when the signals moved
To stop or slow or all clear, and then strain

To catch the oncoming noise around the bend.
Or sometimes for variety I'd perch
Where I could note the make of every car
That passed along the street. Pure research,

Disinterested—but why, and into what?
There was no question then, no answer now.

Why change the memory into metaphors
That solitary child would disavow?

Because

My father and my mother never quarrelled.
They were united in a kind of love
As daily as the *Sydney Morning Herald*,
Rather than like the eagle or the dove.

I never saw them casually touch,
Or show a moment's joy in one another.
Why should this matter to me now so much?
I think it bore more hardly on my mother,

Who had more generous feeling to express.
My father had dammed up his Irish blood
Against all drinking praying fecklessness,
And stiffened into stone and creaking wood.

His lips would make a switching sound, as though
Spontaneous impulse must be kept at bay.
That it was mainly weakness I see now,
But then my feelings curled back in dismay.

Small things can pit the memory like a cyst:
Having seen other fathers greet their sons,
I put my childish face up to be kissed
After an absence. The rebuff still stuns

My blood. The poor man's curt embarrassment
At such a delicate proffer of affection
Cut like a saw. But home the lesson went:
My tenderness thenceforth escaped detection.

My mother sang *Because*, and *Annie Laurie*,
White Wings, and other songs; her voice was sweet.
I never gave enough, and I am sorry;
But we were all closed in the same defeat.

People do what they can; they were good people,
They cared for us and loved us. Once they stood
Tall in my childhood as the school, the steeple.
How can I judge without ingratitude?

Judgment is simply trying to reject
A part of what we are because it hurts.
The living cannot call the dead collect:
They won't accept the charge, and it reverts.

It's my own judgment day that I draw near,
Descending in the past, without a clue,
Down to that central deadness: the despair
Older than any hope I ever knew.

Anne Elder
Farmer Goes Berserk

Perhaps she said, lively at first but once
too often in that softly stubborn voice:
'What kind of a country d'ye call this!'—or
'Pity I can't send for a wee drop of rain
from Home'—and that would be Ballachulish
on Loch Lynne (for the nine hundredth time).
Here, water is khaki and each day a battle
with mouths. Seven, born quick as roses but grown
slowly insupportable with their throats
and itches and grizzles. Two farmed out
(a shame, that) and one in a home,
returned maybe for Christmas and Easter
a frightfully quiet stranger. They kept,
just, the four little girls.

                              Would that be enough?
Rain at last, too much; the spuds
to be got in, tractor on the blink, more
work than feasible for one man with fear
waiting in unopened bills and no rest.

No rest ever from her soft worrying tongue
and that ultimate gnawed bone, no rest within
except in the grog (money ill spent) but oh
the beautiful glad spurt of the grog
                              so that he said
'Shut your trap, woman!' Astoundingly.
With the rabbiting gun. And she slumped
open-mouthed all over the bed and then
the four of them, easy! Sleeping easy
in their bright blood *and* the bloody dog
                              and the excitement
of no fear for the crowning achievement
Him Self...
              By Cripes, we can share it
for one day's wonder in the Stop Press, local.
Was he brute or victim, this assassin?
Or were they simply muddlers, no-hopers
who bred and scrapped together?—who eked out
a widowhood from life behind a veil of gums
in a crazy dump with a cracked iron roof
too remote to be even called infamous.
Now in the darkening puddles of their blood,
briefly limelit, they become neighbours.
Did you ever! He went berserk!
                              Unto Everyman,
according to his worth, acclaim for his labours.

Rosemary Dobson
Cock Crow

Wanting to be myself, alone,
Between the lit house and the town
I took the road, and at the bridge
Turned back and walked the way I'd come.

Three times I took that lonely stretch,
Three times the dark trees closed me round,

The night absolved me of my bonds
Only my footsteps held the ground.

My mother and my daughter slept,
One life behind and one before,
And I that stood between denied
Their needs in shutting-to the door.

And walking up and down the road
Knew myself, separate and alone,
Cut off from human cries, from pain,
And love that grows about the bone.

Too brief illusion! Thrice for me
I heard the cock crow on the hill,
And turned the handle of the door
Thinking I knew his meaning well.

The Major-General

Grounded in Greek he kept the stoic phrase
Ready like a revolver in his drawer,
Ex-army, major-general, could outstare
Weakness, opinion and, at last, old age.
He beat the mischief from his younger son;
His wife grew tremulous, pity and grief
Alike withheld her from protesting speech.

Sustained by shoe-trees, trouser-press and cane—
A rough-cut blackthorn with a silver knob—
He kept his bearing, earned a wide respect,
And envy for his wife. Each morning strolled
About the well-kept garden, cut two flowers,
One for his tweed lapel, and one for her
Laid on the breakfast-table like a threat.

The Apparition

In a room empty of all but the shift of shadow
And a wooden chest, solid, beneath the window—
What is she looking for there, kneeling before it?

She has lifted the heavy lid against the sill
And with both hands she seems to be dipping, sieving
And letting fall the folds of unseen linen.

I know the curve of the head, the hair gathered
In a sweep to the crown, the long fingers,
The arch of the back and the line of sloping shoulders.

Is it grave or swaddling clothes you are after? Tell me.
Can you forgive me, I ask. What should I have done?
Speak to me, turn your face, give me an answer.

She leaves the linen, shuts down the lid and is gone.
I truly believe that I know her. My distaff side:
My mother, hers, and the long line backwards of women.

Each time I hope to be given absolution.

Gwen Harwood
Monday

Kröte sits on the beach at noon
    drinking the blood-red wine.
'Oh how shall I pluck from air some tune
    to match this life of mine?'

A Council notice close at hand
    says liquor is forbidden.
In a damp hollow in the sand
    he keeps his bottle hidden.

A few young mothers come his way.
    They frown at Kröte, jerking
their children past as if to say
    decent men would be working.

Kröte thinks: If I had a child . . .
    and dreams himself a creature
with smoky hair, whose spirit's wild
    as wind, whose inmost nature

mirrors his love. The crowding gulls
        rise, as a dumpy likeness
of Kröte's dream, in spectacles,
        stones them. A wave of sickness

shakes him. The child comes close, and hangs
        over him with a grin,
then with her metal spade she bangs
        sharply on Kröte's shin.

Kröte flinches with pain, and scowls,
        'Mädchen, why do you hit me?'
He grabs the lifted spade. She howls
        'Don't let that bad man get me.'

The women turn from their affairs.
        The vicious child lets loose a
torrent of lies. Her mother glares
        at Kröte like Medusa.

'Monster! You filthy pervert!' scream
        the child-envenomed jury;
round his condemned retreat they seam
        the tissue of their fury.

In vain this night will Kröte try
        on the rinsed beach to find
his wine, or lose the thoughts that lie
        like stains upon his mind.

An Impromptu for Ann Jennings

Sing, memory, sing those seasons in the freezing
        suburb of Fern Tree, a rock-shaded place
with tree ferns, gullies, snowfalls and eye-pleasing
        prospects from paths along the mountain-face.

Nursing our babies by huge fires of wattle,
        or pushing them in prams when it was fine,
exchanging views on diet, or Aristotle,
        discussing Dr Spock or Wittgenstein,

cleaning up infants and the floors they muddied,
    bandaging, making ends and tempers meet—
sometimes I'd mind your children while you studied,
    or you'd take mine when I felt near defeat;

keeping our balance somehow through the squalling
    disorder, or with anguish running wild
when sickness, a sick joke from some appalling
    orifice of the nightwatch, touched a child;

think of it, woman: each of us gave birth to
    four children, our new lords whose beautiful
tyrannic kingdom might restore the earth to
    that fullness we thought lost beyond recall

when, in the midst of life, we could not name it,
    when spirit cried in darkness, '*I will have…*'
but what? have what? There was no word to frame it,
    though spirit beat at flesh as in a grave

from which it could not rise. But we have risen.
    Caesar's we were, and wild, though we seemed tame.
Now we move where we will. Age is no prison
    to hinder those whose joy has found its name.

We are our own. All Caesar's debts are rendered
    in full to Caesar. Time has given again
a hundredfold those lives that we surrendered,
    the love, the fruitfulness; but not the pain.

Before the last great fires we two went climbing
    like gods or blessed spirits in summer light
with the quiet pulse of mountain water chiming
    as if twenty years were one long dreaming night,

above the leafy dazzle of the streams
    to fractured rock, where water had its birth,
and stood in silence, at the roots of dreams,
    content to know: our children walk the earth.

Dialogue

If an angel came with one wish
I might say, deliver that child
who died before birth, into life.
Let me see what she might have become.
He would bring her into a room
fair skinned   the bones of her hands
would press on my shoulderblades
in our long embrace

                                we would sit
with the albums spread on our knees:
now here are your brothers   and here
your sister   here the old house
among trees and espaliered almonds.
    —But where am I?

                                Ah my dear
I have only one picture

                         here
in my head   I saw you lying
still folded   one moment   forever
your head bent down to your heart
eyes closed on unspeakable wisdom
your delicate frog-pale fingers

                              spread
apart as if you were playing
a woodwind instrument.
    —My name?
                        It was never given.
    —Where is my grave?
                      in my head   I suppose
the hospital burnt you.
    —Was I beautiful?
                To me.
    —Do you mourn for me every day?
Not at all   it is more than thirty years
I am feeling the coolness of age

the perspectives of memory change.
Pearlskull   what lifts you here
from night-drift to solemn ripeness?
Mushroom dome? Gourd plumpness?
The frog in my pot of basil?
> — It is none of these, but a rhythm
> the bones of my fingers   dactylic
> rhetoric smashed from your memory.
> Forget me again.
>   Had I lived
> no rhythm would be the same
> nor my brothers and sister feast
> in the world's eternal house.

Overhead   wings of cloud
        burning   and under my feet
            stones marked with demons' teeth.

Mother Who Gave Me Life

Mother who gave me life
I think of women bearing
women. Forgive me the wisdom
I would not learn from you.

It is not for my children I walk
on earth in the light of the living.
It is for you, for the wild
daughters becoming women,

anguish of seasons burning
backward in time to those other
bodies, your mother, and hers
and beyond, speech growing stranger

on thresholds of ice, rock, fire,
bones changing, heads inclining
to monkey bosom, lemur breast,
guileless milk of the word.

I prayed you would live to see
Halley's Comet a second time.
The Sister said, When she died
she was folding a little towel.

You left the world so, having lived
nearly thirty thousand days:
a fabric of marvels folded
down to a little space.

At our last meeting I closed
the ward door of heavy glass
between us, and saw your face
crumple, fine threadbare linen

worn, still good to the last,
then, somehow, smooth to a smile
so I should not see your tears.
Anguish: remembered hours:

a lamp on embroidered linen,
my supper set out, your voice
calling me in as darkness
falls on my father's house.

Nora Krouk
Post Retirement Blues

I live with a man
who is improving his mind:
perched on a swivel chair
he pulls out files
sorts clippings   delves
into Spanish tomes
gets cross with electronic
opponents—the chessboard
blinking over a stalled game.
Above the strewn pages

odd shoes, socks
items of clothing
he follows the flow
of international tensions.
Intention? Why, simply
to sharpen his mind.

He holds unusually
strong opinions
on economics and
modern poetry
(that overrated, pretentious stuff).
I know that arguments
can get rough.

Things whirr
as the phone clamours
casserole simmers
FM sobs lieder.
A line has surfaced:

> For years this dichotomy
> was a blessing…

Switch off the burner!
A shirt needs pressing
Rachmaninoff magic,
sweet smell of baked bread…
Hands picking up things,
a faltering thread.

Shafts of blue air
through the strata of time
chimes   clocks

knives in the kitchen
cut to the bone.

Oodgeroo Noonuccal
Ballad of the Totems

My father was Noonuccal man and kept old tribal way,
His totem was the Carpet Snake, whom none must ever slay;
But mother was of Peewee clan, and loudly she expressed
The daring view that carpet snakes were nothing but a pest.

Now one lived right inside with us in full immunity,
For no one dared to interfere with father's stern decree:
A mighty fellow ten feet long, and as we lay in bed
We kids could watch him round a beam not far above our head.

Only the dog was scared of him, we'd hear its whines and
    growls,
But mother fiercely hated him because he took her fowls.
You should have heard her diatribes that flowed in angry
    torrents
With words you never see in print, except in D. H. Lawrence.

'I kill that robber,' she would scream, fierce as a spotted cat;
'You see that bulge inside of him? My speckly hen make that!'
But father's loud and strict command made even mother quake;
I think he'd sooner kill a man than kill a carpet snake.

That reptile was a greedy-guts, and as each bulge digested
He'd come down on the hunt at night as appetite suggested.
We heard his stealthy slithering sound across the earthen floor,
While the dog gave a startled yelp and bolted out the door.

Then over in the chicken-yard hysterical fowls gave tongue,
Loud frantic squawks accompanied by the barking of the mung,
Until at last the racket passed, and then to solve the riddle,
Next morning he was back up there with a new bulge in his
    middle.

When father died we wailed and cried, our grief was deep and
    sore;
And strange to say from that sad day the snake was seen no
    more.

The wise old men explained to us: 'It was his tribal brother,
And that is why it done a guy'— but some looked hard at
    mother.

She seemed to have a secret smile, her eyes were smug and wary,
She looked as innocent as the cat that ate the pet canary.
We never knew, but anyhow (to end this tragic rhyme)
I think we all had snake for tea one day about that time.

Colour Bar

When vile men jeer because my skin is brown,
This I live down.

But when a taunted child comes home in tears,
Fierce anger sears.

The colour bar! It shows the meaner mind
Of moron kind.

Men are but medieval yet, as long
As lives this wrong.

Could he but see, the colour-baiting clod
Is blaming God

Who made us all, and all His children He
Loves equally.

As long as brothers banned from brotherhood
You still exclude,

The Christianity you hold so high
Is but a lie,

Justice a cant of hypocrites, content
With precedent.

Nan McDonald
The Hatters

The hut in the bush of bark or rusty tin,
The feel of eyes watching, willing you to be gone:
Here lives a hatter. He has done with the world.
Whatever it was in the end he could not bear—
To look in the face of lecher and fool and see
Himself; the rub of the mask on bleeding skin;
The heavy yoke of God, daily put on,
To endure all things and give back love again—
He has chosen the bush, its simpler cruelty,
Its certain peace. I, too, could break the snare,
Take the hatter's path, say no to God and men…
Yet from such an end, good Lord, deliver me.

My grandfather, riding down Araluen way,
A young man then—it is eighty years and more
Since the rocks of those wild hillsides shone for him
In the yellow sun, and the singing river ran
Clear over nuggets of gold—passed carelessly
The humpy hidden in vines from the bright day
And a hatter fired at him from the dark of the door.
Solemn thought—at least, to me, you may laugh if you will—
That if his aim had been better I should not be.
More solemn, that in the end, between man and man,
There is no choice but this: to love or kill.
From the blood of my brother, Lord, deliver me.

Another lived in the sandhills, a sea-lulled hollow,
And raised a sign to ward off peering eyes:
'Beware of the lion.' Any trick was fair against them
But I think he believed it, had seen at morning there
On the rippled beach, through the fine-pricked tracery
Of crab and bird, strange tracks he dared not follow;
Or at twilight, when the silver dune-grass sighs,
Had seen the tawny sand, that slept all day
Warm and quiet, rise up now, move stealthily

About his hut. Still he cries to me, 'Beware!
Beware the beast that lurks along this way!'
From the claws of madness, Lord, deliver me.

And in the mountains behind Jamberoo,
The bush dead still at noon, clouds hanging low,
I came on a hut, close barred, the windows darkened,
On its door one word: 'Silence!' And all around
A hush so deep no sound, it seemed, could be
Unwelcome—the shriek of a black cockatoo
Though it boded storm, the hungry cry of a crow,
Even human speech, so rare in that lost place.
I did not knock; I had no wish to see
One who desired a silence more profound.
What hand would have opened to me there? What face?
From the love of death, dear Lord, deliver me.

Dimitris Tsaloumas
From *Rhapsodic Meditation on the Melbourne Suburb of St Kilda*
Reffo

Stiff with age and recent memories
from the death camps, she'd come
down the stairs, teapot in hand,
and cross the kitchen gloom
with a smile so imponderable
we thought it meant for others,
despite the cupboard-hung walls.
She was fond of black bread
and pickled herring, and talked
of recipes too difficult to test
in the pot. Often the night
was alerted to the sounds
of preparation. She shuffled about
in her balcony room and noises

of opening and shutting, of things
dragged on the floor, would slip
the guard of her discretion. Also,
the rustle of paper and hushed,
torn words. She'd found the sun
too strong in this country,
the family bonds too loose.
I was refused time off to attend
the funeral. She was neither relative
nor friend but she didn't go
beyond the vague periphery
of my living, where shadows lurk
and break through secret gaps
to body forth their bitter meaning.

Geoffrey Dutton
A Finished Gentleman

*'In the distant desert you unexpectedly stumble on a finished
gentleman.'*

Captain George Grey, *Journals of Two Expeditions of Discovery*

Under the white silence of the great gumtree avenue
My parents taught me to be an English gentleman,
And a thousand galahs rose like petals thrown at the sunset,
Swearing like the native Australians they are. Bastards! Bastards!
Yet no one more legitimate than I, whose ancestors
Planted the trees and houses here where no one had planted
Even a seed, or penned a sheep, or dammed a creek.
No style grows out of nothingness, droughts and scabby sheep
Teach patience but not manners, and so it was 1900,
And the second generation, and there was Grandfather,
    gleaming,
The Squire of Anlaby, with a steam yacht, RYS,
Fourteen gardeners, and silver-gilt candlesticks for the church
    he was building.

And so with Oxford, rowing, and maybe the Diplomatic in
    view,
I grew among grass seeds and dust storms and later, in the scent
Of the distillery wafting across the Eton of Corio Bay,
Being expert at coping with visiting Governors and their
    intolerable ADCs.
And their ladies (though once I shot one of these in the bottom
    with an arrow)
Could tell a Holland and Holland from a Greener, English
    cloth from Australian,

Knew the Wars of the Roses but had scarcely heard of Eureka,
Could decline Omnis Gallia into any number of parts,
And after chanting 'Alpha Beta Gamma Delta,
Knock a lady down and belt her,' learned to read
In Greek the speech of an Athenian lawyer in a dispute over
    drains,
Though I knew nothing of Bligh or Macarthur, Parkes or
    Deakin,
Could tell you the agonies of Xenophon, Livingstone, and
    someone up the Amazon,
But nothing of Sturt down the Murray, or Eyre across the
    Nullarbor,
Knew the *Revenge* and the *Golden Hind*, but not *Sirius* or the
    Endeavour.

And yet, in the coach-house I ran my finger over the acetylene
    lamps
Of my father's 1908 Talbot, first car driven across Australia,
Walked through the mulgas my mother had brought back from
    the Territory,
Grilled chops on gum-sticks, caught yabbies, had the slippery
    bumps
Of a rabbit's guts often in my hand, loved Australia passionately
As did my father and mother in between reading
The Illustrated London News, The Cornhill, Britannia and Eve.

And what did it give me, to be an Austroenglish gentleman?
A torment of comparative values, nothing here so old, so rare,
So fine. Trivial despairs at people who drank sweet wine,
Sat on Genoa velvet, walked in square-capped shoes,
Talked of nothing but marks, furlongs, overs, of dagoes and
    reffos,
Of long-hairs and sissies, the wisdom of the ordinary, decent
    bloke.

Well, as I look back, I was indeed a finished gentleman.
Twenty years to learn to be one, twenty years and more
To learn what Jack or Mick knew all the time, that here
It is we live, unless we pretend, or run away.

But hold it! The galahs are thicker than they ever were,
Four thousand marvellous sunset flowers tumbling
On to the shredded upper stalks of the great white trees.
Bastards! Bastards! they scream. Yes, Jack and Mick
Were ignorant bastards in another way. Maybe they could
    whittle
Myall stockwhip handles and ride straight home through the
    maze
Of mallee, and roll their own and recite all of 'The Sick
    Stockrider',
But this landscape was not cleared by such sweet simplicities
    alone,
And their bright axes would bounce off the rubbery jungle
Of ideas never thought necessary in this innocent country.
And, educated down, I still know the world's crooked hours are
    different
From the hands around me, raising schooners at closing time.

Dorothy Hewett
Legend of the Green Country

I

September is the spring month bringing tides, swilling green in
the harbour mouth,

Turnabout dolphins rolling-backed in the rip and run, the king
waves

Swinging the coast, snatching at fishermen from Leeuwin to
Norah's Head;

A dangerous month: but I count on an abacus as befits a shop-
keeper's daughter.

I never could keep count by modern methods, the ring of the
till

Is profit and loss, the ledger, hasped with gold, sits in its heavy
dust

On the counter, out front the shopkeeper's sign hangs loose and
bangs in the wind,

The name is obliterated, the dog swells and stinks in the gutter,

The golden smell of the beer does not run in the one street, like
water,

The windmill head hangs, broken-necked, flapping like a great
plain turkey

As the wind rises…this was my country, here I go back for
nurture

To the dry soaks, to the creeks running salt through the timber,

To the ghosts of the sandalwood cutters, and the blue breath of
their fires,

To the navvies in dark blue singlets laying rails in the scrub.

My grandfather rode out, sawing at a hard-mouthed ginger
horse,

And a hard heart in him, a dray full of rum and beer, bully-beef
and treacle,

Flour and tea, workboots and wide-awakes with the corks
bobbing for flies;

Counting the campfires in the dusk, counting the men,
   counting the money,
Counting the sheep from the goats, and the rack-rented railway
   houses.
No wonder I cannot count for the sound of the money-
   changers,
The sweat and the clink, the land falling into the cash register,
Raped and eroded, thin and black as a myall girl on a railway
   siding.

He came back, roaring and singing up from the gullies, his
   beard
Smelt of rum, his moneybag plump as a wild duck under his
   saddle.
The old horse stumbled in the creek bed but brought him
   home,
The dray rattled; as they took him down in the yard he cursed
   and swore
At the dream, and blubbered for it: next Saturday night he rode
   his horse
Up the turkey red carpet into the bar, smashing the bottles and
   glasses,
Tipping the counter, sending the barmaid screaming, her breasts
   tilting with joy.
The great horse reared and he sang and swore and flung his hat
   at the sky,
And won his bets, and rode home, satisfied, to a nagging wife
   and daughter,
Having buried his pain and his lust under the broken bottles.

The publican swept them up in the cold light next morning,
And that was the end of it, they thought, but it wasn't so easy:
There is no end to it and I stand at the mole watching the sea
   run out,
Or hang over the rails at the Horseshoe Bridge and listen to the
   tide,
Listen to the earth that pleasured my grandfather with his flocks
   and acres

Drowned under salt, his orange trees forked bare as unbreeched
   boys.
Only the apples, little and hard, bitten green and bitter as salt,
They come up in the spring, in the dead orchard they are the
   fruit
 Of our knowledge, and I am Eve, spitting the pips in the eye of
   the myth-makers.

This is my legend; an old man on a ginger horse who filled his
   till
And died content with a desert, or so they said: his stone angel
Cost a pretty penny, but the workmanship was faulty, its wings
   curve
In a great arc over the graveyard, it grows mildewed and dirty,
Its nose is syphilitic, its feet splay like a peasant, its hands
Clasp over its breast like the barmaid who screamed in the pub,
And kissed him, for love, not money, but only once.

II

My grandmother had a bite like a sour green apple,
Little and pitiless she kept the till,
Counted the profits, and stacked the bills of sale.
She bought the shops and the farms, the deeds were hers,
In the locked iron safe with a shower of golden sovereigns.
She never trusted the banks, they failed in the nineties,
She kept her banknotes rolled in the top of her stocking,
Caressingly, while her prices soared and dropped,
Her barometer; crops and wool and railway lines.
Each night she read the news by the hurricane lantern,
While the only child wept for love in the washing-up water.
She could argue like a man, politics, finance, banking.
In her rocking chair with her little dangling feet,
Her eyes glittered like broken beer bottle glass.
She kept one eye out for a farmer to spend his money
And a sharp tongue for a borrowing mate of my grandfather's.

Once, long ago, in Swanston Street she 'made'
For fashionable ladies, their breasts half bared
And their ankles covered, pads in their hair,
Bustles, bugle beads and jet, dyed ostrich feathers,
You could see their shadows waving from hansom cabs,
And the ghostly wheels turning into Swanston Street.
She had her miracles and quoted them...
Science and Health by Mary Baker Eddy,
She read the *Monitor* while the dust storms whirled,
And marvelled that God was love; it was all clear profit.
She wet the bagging to filter the westerlies,
Planted geraniums and snowdrops under the tank,
And squashed black caterpillars on moonlit forays.
She balanced the ledger and murmured, 'God is love,'
Feeling like God, she foreclosed on another farm.

She never read for pleasure, or danced or sang,
Or listened with love, slowly life smote her dumb,
Till she lay in the best bedroom, pleating the quilt,
In a fantasy of ball dresses for Melbourne ladies.
Her eyes were remote as pennies, her sheets stank,
She cackled and counted a mythical till all her days.

III

My father was a black-browed man who rode like an Abo.
The neighbours gossiped, 'A touch of the tarbrush there.'
He built the farm with his sweat, it lay in the elbow
Of two creeks, thick with wattle and white tea-tree.
At night he blew on the cornet; once, long ago, he'd played
On the pleasure cruises that went up the Yarra on Saturday
    nights;
The lights bobbed in the muddy water, the girls in white muslin
    sang 'Tipperary'.
Now he played in the lonely sleep-out, looking out over the flat,
With the smell of creek water, and a curlew crying like a
    murdered gin,

Crying all night, till he went out with a shotgun and finished its
    screaming,
But not his own…he, the mendicant, who married the store-
    keeper's daughter.

My mother was a dark round girl in a country town,
With down on her lip, her white cambric blouse
Smelt of roses and starch, she was beautiful,
Warm, and frigid in a world of dried-up women,
Aborting themselves with knitting needles on farms.
She wept in the tin humpy at the back of the store,
For the mother who hated, the father who drank
And loved her; then, sadly, she fell in love
And kissed the young accountant who kept the books,
Behind the ledgers, the summer dust on the counters.
He was on the booze, broke all his promises,
Went off to the city and sang in an old spring cart,
'Bottle-oh, Bottle-oh' till his liver gave out
And he died; she married in arum lilies, satin, tulle,
Under the bell that tolled for the storekeeper's daughter.
Men shot themselves in the scrub on her wedding day.
My father brought her wildflowers, rode forty miles,
But he never kissed like the beautiful bottle-oh,
Boozing in the pub like a fly caught in its amber.

The roof of the hospital cracked like purgatory,
At sunset the birth blood dried on the sheets,
Nobody came to change them, the sun went down,
The pain fell on her body like a beast and mauled it.

She hated the farm, hated the line of wattles
Smudging the creek, kept her hands full of scones,
Boiled the copper, washing out sins in creek water,
Kept sex at bay like the black snake coiled in the garden.
Burning under the African daisies and bridal creeper,
Took her children to bed, he lay alone in the sleep-out,
With a headache and *The Seven Pillars of Wisdom*.

The girls in their picture hats came giggling and singing,
Trailing their hands like willows from the Yarra launches,
Till the dream was nightmare and all his life a regret,
Bought and gelded in an old grey house by a creek bed.

Anniversary

Death is in the air—

today is the anniversary of his death in October
(he would have been thirty-one)
I went home to High Street
& couldn't feed the new baby
my milk had dried up
so I sat holding him numbly
looking for the soft spot on the top of his head
while they fed me three more librium
you're only crying for yourself he said
but I kept on saying *It's the waste I can't bear.*

All that winter we lived
in the longest street in the world
he used to walk to work in the dark
on the opposite side of the street
somebody always walked with him but they never met
he could only hear the boots
& when he stopped they stopped.

The new baby swayed in a canvas cot lacing his fingers
I worried in case he got curvature of the spine
Truby King said a baby needed firm support
he was a very big bright baby
the cleaner at the Queen Vic said every morning
you mark my words that kid's been here before.

The house was bare & cold with a false gable
we had no furniture only a double mattress
on the floor a big table & two deal chairs

each morning I dressed the baby in a shrunken jacket
& caught the bus home to my mother's to nurse the child
who was dying   the house had bay windows
hidden under fir trees smothered in yellow roses
the child sat dwarfed at the end of the polished table
pale as death in the light of his four candles
singing 'Little Boy Blue'.

I pushed the pram to the telephone box
I'm losing my milk I told her   *I want to bring him
home to die   Home* she said   *you left
home a long time ago to go with that man.*

I pushed them both through the park
over the dropped leaves (his legs were crippled)
a magpie swooped down black out of the sky
& pecked his forehead   a drop of blood splashed on
his wrist   he started to cry

It took five months & everybody was angry
because the new baby was alive & cried for attention
pollen sprinkled his cheeks under the yellow roses.

When he died it was like everybody else
in the public ward with the screens around him
the big bruises spreading on his skin
his hand came up out of the sheets *don't cry*
he said   *don't be sad*
I sat there overweight in my Woolworth's dress
not telling anybody in case they kept him alive
with another transfusion—

        Afterwards I sat by the gas fire
in my old dressing-gown turning over the photographs
wondering why I'd drunk all that stout
& massaged my breasts every morning to be
        a good mother.

Norma Bloom
The Inheritance

Do not be confused by the lawyer's words—
'…the house on the hill and its acres of lawns,
providing you do not marry or sub-let
and/or remove the pictures on the walls.'

Your inheritance is a debt.
You have been left your father's house of stone,
a garden of oxalis
and a black box playing the minuet.

Your only recourse is to suffer
but not submit,
except in death.

David Rowbotham
The Bus-Stop on the Somme
BENJAMIN HOPPER 1896–1965

Even if you are killed, you die.
My uncle, who survived the Somme,
died waiting at a bus-stop, as though,
in the repeated boom
of mud-wheeled guns, he had at last
been accurately shelled,
shattered by a deep unburied blast.
He died as though he had been killed.

Others at the bus-stop heard the boom.
It cannoned the act of living through
the trenches where we bury the Somme:
and the others waiting knew
the dead go on, don't stop at death
but go as my uncle did
that day on the accurate mud-wheeled earth,
when the shrapnel missed another's head.

Vincent Buckley

Stroke

I

In the faint blue light
We are both strangers; so I'm forced to note
His stare that comes moulded from deep bone,
The full mouth pinched in too far, one hand
Climbing an aluminium bar.
Put, as though for the first time,
In a cot from which only a hand escapes,
He grasps at opposites, knowing
This room's a caricature of childhood.
'I'm done for.'

'They're treating you all right?'
We talk from the corners of our mouths
Like old lags, while his body strains
To notice me, before he goes on watching
At the bed's foot
His flickering familiars,
Skehan, Wilson, Ellis, dead men, faces,
Bodies, paused in the aluminium light,
Submits his answer to his memories,
'Yes, I'm all right. But still it's terrible.'

Words like a fever bring
The pillar of cloud, pillar of fire
Travelling the desert of the mind and face.
The deep-set, momentarily cunning eyes
Keep trying for a way to come
Through the bed's bars to his first home.
And almost find it. Going out I hear
Voices calling requiem, where the cars
Search out the fog and gritty snow,
Hushing its breathing under steady wheels.
Night shakes the seasonable ground.

II

Decorous for the dying's sake
The living talk with eyes and hands
Of football, operations, work;
The pussyfooting nurses take
Their ritual peep; the rule demands

I stand there with a stiff face
Ready, at a word or gleam,
To conjure off the drops of sweat.
So small a licit breathing-space
Brings each inside the other's dream.

Across the bright unechoing floors
The trolleys and attendants rove;
On tiptoe shine, by scoured walls,
The neatly speechless visitors
Skirt the precipice of love.

III

Oaks, pines, the willows with their quiet
Terror; the quiet terror of my age;
The seven-year-old bookworm sitting out
At night, in the intense cold, the horse
Tethered, the stars almost moving,
The cows encroaching on the night grass.
The frost stung my lips; my knees burned;
Darkness alone was homely. The hawthorn tree
Glimmered as though frost had turned to language
And language into sharp massy blossoms.
Once, I even scraped my father's hand
And glimpsed the white underside of poplars
That, moving, almost touched the flashing stars.
Squat, steep-browed, the Methodist Church nestled
Halfway between the distant police station
And the near barn; a whole world

Gave neither words nor heat, but merely
A geometry of the awakening sight.

I had forgotten that night, or nights;
And if I think back, there's nothing mythical:
A cross-legged kid with a brooding nose
His hands were too chilled to wipe,
A book whose pages he could hardly turn.
A silent father he had hardly learned
To touch; cold he could bear,
Though chill-blooded; the dark heat of words.
A life neither calm nor animal.
Now, in the deeper quiet of my age,
I feel thirty years
Turning my blood inwards; neither trees nor stars,
But a hush and start of traffic; spasms of sound
Loosening tram rails, bluestone foundations,
Manuscripts, memories; too many tasks;
A body shrinking round its own
Corruption, though a long way from dying.
We suit our memories to our sufferings.

IV

Every clod reveals an ancestor.
They, the spirit hot in their bodies,
Burned to ash in their own thoughts; could not
Find enough water; rode in a straight line
Twenty miles across country
For hatred jumping every wire fence;
With uillean pipes taunted the air
Ferociously that taunted them;
Spoke with rancour, but with double meanings;
Proud of muscle, hated the bone beneath;
Married to gain forty acres
And a family of bond servants; died bound.
I, their grandson, do not love straight lines,
And talk with a measured voice—in double meanings—

Remembering always, when I think of death,
The grandfather, small, loveless, sinister,
['The most terrible man I ever seen',
Said Joe, who died thin as rice paper]
Horse-breaker, heart-breaker, whose foot scorches,
Fifty years after, the green earth of Kilmore.
It's his heat that lifts my father's frame
Crazily from the wheel-chair, fumbles knots,
Twists in the bed at night,
Considers every help a cruelty.

V

Indoors and out, weather and winds keep up
Time's passion: paddocks white for burning.
As usual, by his bed, I spend my time
Not in talk, but restless noticing:
If pain dulls, grief coarsens.
Each night we come and, voyeurs of decay,
Stare for minutes over the bed's foot,
Imagining, if we think at all,
The body turning ash, the near insane
Knowledge when, in the small hours,
Alone under the cold ceiling, above
The floor where the heating system keeps its pulse,
He grows accustomed to his own sweat
And sweats with helplessness, remembering
How, every day, at eight o'clock
The Polish nurse kisses him goodnight.
His arms are bent like twigs; his eyes
Are blown to the door after her; his tears
Are squeezed out not even for himself.
Where is the green that swells against the blade
Or sways in sap to the high boughs? To the root
He is dry wood, and in his sideways
Falling brings down lights. Our breath
Mingles,
Stirs the green air of the laurel tree.

VI

The roofs are lit with rain.
Winter. In that dark glow,
Now, as three months ago,
I pray that he'll die sane.

On tiles or concrete path
The old wheeling the old,
For whom, in this last world,
Hope is an aftermath,

And the damp trees extend
Branch and thorn. We live
As much as we believe.
All things covet an end.

Once, on the Kerrie road,
I drove with him through fire.
Now, in the burnt cold year,
He drains off piss and blood.

His wounded face tube-fed,
His arm strapped to a bed.

VII

At the merest handshake I feel his blood
Move with the ebb-tide chill. Who can revive
A body settled in its final mood?
To whom, on what tide, can we move, and live?

Later I wheel him out to see the trees:
Willows and oaks, the small plants he mistakes
For rose bushes; and there
In front, looming, light green, cypresses.
His pulse no stronger than the pulse of air.

Dying, he grows more tender, learns to teach
Himself the mysteries I am left to trace.
As I bend to say 'Till next time', I search
For signs of resurrection in his face.

Jill Hellyer
Living with Aunts

I

Passed to two maiden aunts, the quiet child
absorbed the trinity of their beliefs;
only in adolescence she learned to cry
and later, much later, to analyse her griefs.

Her thoughts were tracts they never visited:
the child became myself, always unknown
but present, obedient, silent. I watched them eat
slowly, talk slowly, and the seeds were sown

of the divinity of the *Sydney Morning Herald*,
the British Empire, and the ABC:
I was always told how fortunate I was
as though my needs were met by literacy.

My aunt once saw reviewed in her Saturday *Herald*
The Rise and Fall of the British Empire. She
read it to us in helpless disbelief.
(It wasn't mentioned on the ABC)

2

I'd always thought Soames Forsyte was a cousin,
I'd heard so much about him. One aunt read
all of the Saga, the other had poor eyesight
so she and I both painstakingly were fed

news of the Forsytes slowly at the table.
I knew Soames better than I knew my father
whose death I learned about in secret from
a *Herald* clipping. I was the child left over.

3

I was always a bother to them, and they'd say
You're not a proper Hellyer, not with brown eyes
(as though it were a crime). I was the wrong
dreamer of wrong dreams, was the wrong size,

never came first in the class for them nor brandished
my energy for causes they considered noble.
But the British Empire after all had fallen
too while they ate so slowly at the table.

J. R. Rowland
Family Happiness

Family happiness
A theme not much explored
Left aside as lacking
Conflict, movement, stress—

Instead, the pangs of search
Among people who seldom seem
To marry, have regular jobs
Or go to dentist or church,

And are rarely over thirty.
Falling in and out of love
In a kind of prolonged weekend
They don't pay bills, wash dirty

Socks, mend plugs, mow lawns
Nor cut the children's lunches
But drink whisky or campari
Converse in restaurants

Or agonize alone
On a range of subjects that
Leaves untouched what you
Or I flinch from as our own

Inmost fear or distress.
The world of novels is
Autonomous, it seems.
That it does not come too close

May be just as well
When, the children being in bed,

I see your reading head
In the quiet of lightfall,

Your eye stumble, and quick
Pierce mine with a glance
Where something unbearable rises
Trembles and sinks back.

Joan Mas
The Widow

The widow who lives in a house at the end of the street
      has a lover
And an illegitimate child. She is fenced about by the long
      sharp tongues of people.
Every day a new picket is added to the fence.
Neighbours have a way of extending it. Women over tea-cups.
      Men, over garden-walls.
That the widow has found an exit in the fence and walks
      through it
With the child, indicates a weakness in its structure. Some
      faltering of will, by someone…
          somewhere,
Has made a gap between pickets.
The widow who never glances at people, keeps them suspiciously
      glancing at one another.

Barrett Reid
Marie at Saint-Cloud

You took my hands and night fell.
Around the library where we sat
the house was full of ordinary sounds,
the children gone to bed still chattering,
Milly clearing up, closing windows,
my husband's footsteps fading down the hall.
You took my hands, spoke quietly.

My husband went away along the hall,
his footfall echoing in my mind
its soft departing sound, and I
heard nothing quite the same way ever again,
not the children's cries, nor the house—its noises,
doors opening, closing, nor my lover's voice,
never the same again.

Bruce Beaver

'Remembering Golden Bells'
...and Po Chu-I

I

This was the daughter regretfully begotten
In your fortieth year.
    Having made it plain
In several lines of inimitable verse
How commonplace a joy and unpardonable
In fatherhood when girl is not boy,
Such tendencies to ache with old laughter
At her lispings, wake to a new wonder
At her charmed comings and goings, you accepted her
With heartfelt thanks and due reservations
As back-to-front convention bade you.
                 Then
Suddenly she went out of your life
And her own, leaving you at forty-one
Lacking a daughter, no more than bereft,
Less than alone, yet in pain.

II

Sequels are obvious, delight in telling us
Where we fell short of grasping the true
Fruit of the tree's one meaning,
Of taking to head and heart another's labour

Of love consumed and indigestible.
In this way books come back to us
Twice telling themselves and going unread
For all their painful growing, we having bitten
Off unwisely more than we can chew
This once, and become doubly shy.

III

But there are sequels, otherwise unsought,
Met with among the living: the returning
Sense of absence, the complete work of loss.
After three years, suddenly meeting
In an unfamiliar street her foster-nurse,
You found yourself again at the beginning
Of her brief book, reading over your grief,
Knowing sequels inescapable
And, though unsought, with terrible compassion
Finding these—the laughter and the wonder—
In retrospect more harrowing than tears.

From *Letters to Live Poets*
X

The sou'wester whips the day awake.
The pines are tossing 'monkey tails'
about the gardens and the streets.
The air hums and rushes overhead
and next-door the little girl
is calling out to it.
All week she has blown
a two-note whistle and called the tune
her own. The white and blue weather
excites her. The wind blows
back into her face the tune.
She catches it and feels it blown
about her hair and face.

It buzzes like wild bees;
it stings with specks of dust and sand.
Yet over it and under it is the cool
to warmer charm of the September breeze,
spiked with salt and mellowed with
the mild juice of new grass.

The sheets crack and flap a semaphore
among the red and blue and black of 'coloureds'.
She sits cross-legged beneath
the carousel of washing, fluting
and singing two notes, two words:
'I am, I am'. The mother
admonishes. She is thin and sallow,
without a man. Has her reasons
all about her like an angry
counterpoint. All winter
she has yelled at the child who yells
back at herself 'I am, I am'.
But the devas of the air and sky
respond 'We are, we are' and lift her
over the yards and the thrumming pines,
past gargling crows and creaking gulls,
above the splintering enamel
of the blue and whitening bay
back to where she is with a man
out of the clouds. The 'he' who'll spank
her mother good and bring them all
toffee apples every day.

How she sings and makes the whistle
talk to her. When she goes
inside the house her hair will crackle
and float about. Her mother will lick
the corner of a handkerchief
and clean the corners of her eyes.
Then by herself again
she'll clean the whistle's gritty mouth

and listen to it humming to
itself.
    Do you hear them now?
Have I admitted something past
my manhood? Do we recollect
blowing up a sunny storm
all by ourselves once upon
a time in a backyard garden
near the sea?
Or is it that all women
learn to sing to themselves early
that some men, early or late,
may listen?

R. F. Brissenden
Building a Terrace

Sentimental nonsense of course to talk
Of the 'living rock' or the 'honesty' of stone—
But the words are in my mind each time I dig
Some stubborn chunk of sandstone out of the earth,
Split, dress and settle it into place
In wall or terrace; and I think of two dead men:
My grandfather Will Rogers, and Archimedes.
'Give me a lever,' he said, 'and I'll shift the world.'
Rocks that a man can't lift can smash a foot—
And when, after crowbar, shovel and mattock have done
Their work, you feel a big stone gently tilt
And shift at a sweating finger's touch you know
In your bones what the old Greek meant. Archimedes
May have been just a name to Grandad, but
He loved stone and worked it till he died.
Seventy-five he was and stood as straight
As when he'd landed thirty years before
With his box of tools, his family and his lodge
Certificate: Oddfellows Master at Bridgnorth
In Shropshire—*Amicitia, amor*

Et veritas beneath the eye of God.
In Sydney it meant nothing. But he worked:
Anonymous flagged paths, hearths, terraces,
Fireplaces that draw and walls that stand
Are his memorial. He whistled, sang,
Was gentle, smelled of mortar, sawdust, sweat
And the open air. 'Drunk again,' he'd say,
Laughing under old-fashioned moustaches when
I fell running to watch him split the stone.
He was an artist—he could knock a tune
Out of an old tin can, they said—and when
His sledge-hammer rang on his steel wedges the rock
Broke clean and straight. I touched the fresh
Rock-faces that had never seen the sun.
At home, he said, sinking a well they found
A frog alive inside a hollow rock
Ten feet beneath the ground. He built a wall
The day before he died—surprised by death
Like that old man in Syracuse who fell
Under the ignorant Roman soldier's spear
Face down across his drawings in the sand.

Peter Porter
Somme and Flanders

Who am I to speak up for the long dead?
Three uncles I never knew say I'm right.
Their tongues are speaking in my head
I'm related to their flesh by fright.

Their world was made of nerves and mud.
Reading about it now shocks me—Haig
Gets transfusions of their blood,
Plum-and-apple feeds them for the plague.

Those Harmsworth books have sepia'd
Their peasants' fields sown with barbed-wire.

In Nineteen-Nineteen, crops of crosses appeared
Seeded by bodies ripened in shell-fire.

One image haunts us who have read of death
In Auschwitz in our time—it is just light,
Shivering men breathing rum crouch beneath
The sandbag parapet—left to right

The line goes up and over the top,
Serious in gas masks, bayonets fixed,
Slowly forward—the swearing shells have stopped—
Somewhere ahead of them death's stop-watch ticks.

Family Album

Tenable in dreams, here they are twice
as plausible, holding court to the lens,
with nothing to say but the truth.
    Myself, my mother,
culled from the caucus of summer
by a relative's whim: how did the fat woman
keep so many bees off her howling son?
    That man, chained to
his gross watch, wearing his waistcoat
like Prometheus his rock, did he edge
to the aerodrome to show he was too
frightened to enter the twentieth century?
    It makes a good fiction
to leer at their confidence. Something else
would fit in. The light, acid but milky,
along the near shore and the ironclad ferry
touching the stage; Cousin Timperley
walking an ice-cream up to the pines,
Beethoven for supper, everyone upright.
    Later, dispersal may offer
your motorcade stopping en route to Tiberias,
'This is Cana, so don't check the water
in your radiator'. Over us looms Mount

Gilboa where Saul fell on his sword,
a mortar lob from the red hibiscus
kibbutz, its blond children playing
through the collective afternoon.
                    Pictures from a lost
exhibition. Not the pianola and
the telescope, but a high-backed
Russian chair and the brilliantined
bridegroom asleep after venery.
Or this tribute: 'How we brought
the Good News', key of F Minor,
the house in the corn.
                    That hand, that brown face,
now papery, channelled with heart
disease, the transit of Venus.
Mother and father met here in me
ascribing a terror of photographs
to the lingering snake in the garden.
                    Made objective now
on the lake where the red-eyed fish
walk on wallpaper. O sails of death
that we watched on the river, weeks of rain
when we came to our father's house,
the pictures are ready, shall we walk in?

Where We Came In

I collected my father's possessions,
a half-sovereign case, a gold watch,
fourteen carat only, my mother's rings,
and walked into the breathing sun,
                    Another heat shield gone.

Fine powder of selfishness along
my upper lip, the time of jacaranda falling,
here where I was born, the cycle
not yet complete but estrangement
                    Made absolute by time.

I tacked to the car as if I were drunk.
Indeed, I had lost my common sense
of ownership: when inheritance shrinks
to memory and thirty cents in cash,
                    Who's then the family man?

Yet soon in the bar above the cricket field
I rallied, due to timely punishment.
At last I was alone with incandescence
and did not question the mystery,
                    The son was now the father.

The Second Husband

He was a selfless man, beautiful
In all his actions if not handsome in
Himself—look through all his Orders, The Finn,
The Swede, The Turk; powers from Istanbul
To Christiana honoured him, a pin
To wear before the Emperor, a four-
starred crucifix, a jewelled watch the twin
Of Baron Swieten's—I keep them in a drawer.

Marrying him, I swam away from need.
The servants stopped their answering back, the bills
Arrived with presents; I discovered skills
I didn't know I had; the Court agreed
My figures for back pay; the last quadrilles
Sold first, those manuscripts I had to hand
He saw I wasn't cheated on; the quills
We never washed, the ink dried in its stand.

He was the most magnanimous of men,
One sign of it, I ceased my pregnancies.
Those days have long since gone; I have to please
New waves of pilgrims asking how and when.
My sister-in-law and I like two old trees
Live side by side; each plays the oracle.
Her mind is on those childhood prophecies,
Mine on the man who rescued me from hell.

And my misunderstood much-loved second
Husband wrote my first's biography:
I wondered at such generosity.
Now Europe listens, for the world is fecund
And everyone forgets reality
And praises the most marvellous of boys
Who drew the face of God for all to see
But was to me puerility and noise.

R. A. Simpson
The Telephone's Working Again

Two days my telephone's been defunct;
I couldn't dial out
and the world couldn't dial in,
gossip, ask for my kind of truth,
describe angels drifting over the Dandenongs.

Now the line's been corrected,
melting my ivory tower like ice,
and I listen to my mother saying,
'You have a brother born years before
I knew your father—who didn't know.'

Two fathers buried.
An old lie sleepless with her in her single bed.

Bruce Dawe
Condolences of the Season
TO MY SON (BORN DECEMBER 1964)

And now it seems that you and I, my son,
must suffer with like fortitude
the diddums chorus, the ickle-man alleluia,
together with such other ritual oddments
as maiden aunt and grand-dam can devise...

For months to come

your crabbed infant-elderly countenance
must be mulled over to the tea-cup's chink,
a matronly cosmogony of mums
hover above your pram or basinette
and by an infallible process of recall
place each distinctive trait (the eyes, for instance,
which could only be Uncle Tom's, nobody else's,
Aunt Lena's rugged chin, of course and, yes,
who could mistake those ears of Cousin Ted's?)

Identi-Kitted out as fulsomely
as the most Wanted criminal, any means
you choose to shake them off are bound to fail
—bearded, double-chinned, dark-spectacled,
the hair grown long and thatching tell-tale ears,
cheeks padded with the lard of middle-age
—you'll fancy the trail cold, the pack confused,
until, at a family reunion, some frail
octogenarian creature, screaming out,
'How could I be so foolish? Harry's nose!'
shaking with recognition pulls you down…

Lapped in a bunny-rug, you stare them out
and, smarter than they realize, play it dumb,
while, slung for burping purposes across
your mother's shoulder, all is well I see,
catching your droll heretical wink at me…

Drifters

One day soon he'll tell her it's time to start packing,
and the kids will yell 'Truly?' and get wildly excited for no
    reason,
and the brown kelpie pup will start dashing about, tripping
    everyone up,
and she'll go out to the vegetable-patch and pick all the green
    tomatoes from the vines,
and notice how the oldest girl is close to tears because she was
    happy here,

and how the youngest girl is beaming because she wasn't.
And the first thing she'll put on the trailer will be the
    bottling-set
                        she never unpacked from Grovedale,
and when the loaded ute bumps down the drive past the
                        blackberry-canes with their last shrivelled fruit,
she won't even ask why they're leaving this time, or where they're
                        heading for
—she'll only remember how, when they came here,
she held out her hands bright with berries,
the first of the season, and said:
'Make a wish, Tom, make a wish.'

Homecoming

All day, day after day, they're bringing them home,
they're picking them up, those they can find, and bringing them
    home,
they're bringing them in, piled on the hulls of Grants, in trucks,
    in convoys,
they're zipping them up in green plastic bags,
they're tagging them now in Saigon, in the mortuary coolness
they're giving them names, they're rolling them out of
the deep-freeze lockers—on the tarmac at Tan Son Nhut
the noble jets are whining like hounds,
they are bringing them home
—curly-heads, kinky-hairs, crew-cuts, balding non-coms
—they're high, now, high and higher, over the land, the
    steaming *chow mein*
their shadows are tracing the blue curve of the Pacific
with sorrowful quick fingers, heading south, heading east,
home, home, home—and the coasts swing upward, the old
    ridiculous curvatures
of earth, the knuckled hills, the mangrove-swamps, the desert
    emptiness…
in their sterile housing they tilt towards these like skiers
—taxiing in, on the long runways, the howl of their

homecoming rises
surrounding them like their last moments (the mash, the
    splendour)
then fading at length as they move
on to small towns where dogs in the frozen sunset
raise muzzles in mute salute,
and on to cities in whose wide web of suburbs
telegrams tremble like leaves from a wintering tree
and the spider grief swings in his bitter geometry
—they're bringing them home, now, too late, too early.

'Some Village-Hampden...'
a local incident

Out bagging up potatoes in a paddock,
the sun reminding him it stood at zenith,
saw the wife running to him from the house,
and, 'Oh, God, what now?' left bagging-needle and twine
to stomp down red clod rows to find out what.
In the kitchen stared at the cane-lashed back
of Karl, ten, and felt blunt fingers twitch
with all of a blurred passion bagging spuds
was but poor preparation for...
Late afternoon strode into the *Cheyenne*,
grasped the schoolmaster by the neck and said,
'You must be the original child-basher. I'll give you
the same treatment,' lifted him from his chair
and threw him to the floor.

Arrested,
had his day in court, was fined, and told from the bench
that a teacher stood *in loco parentis* (whatever that meant),
and that there were, of late,
far too many cases of this kind...

Returning home, said,
'He beat my kid, so I beat him
—That's all there is to it.'

Philip Martin
Nursing Home

Incontinence, and the mind going. Where?
The place is all it should be. Not enough.
She's had such spirit. *No more advice, thank you!*
And she'd slam down the receiver. Hated drudging:
*The house is crawling away with dirt, but I'm
Going out to garden.* Thwarted, self-thwarted:
Gave up the piano when her marriage failed,
Should have had a career. Instead she moved:
Twenty houses in forty years. And always
Well, dear son, at last we've found the right one.
Never. And now, this one room, to be shared
With a woman still as a stonefish.

                              Sunday morning:
Outside, the trees wrestle with spring wind.
She sits here in her chair beating her tray:
Sister sister sister sister sister!
Clenches her lips, hums against them. And again
Sister sister sister sister sister!
High, scratched voice. *Behind me behind me behind me!*
What is, Mother? A pause. *I don't know.*
And again the drumming: *Sister sister sister!*

                     *

The mind going, and coming back, and going.
Each ebb, a little further. She says one evening
A bit flat today. Long pause, and then
I don't like this place. (What is *this place*?)
And slowly: *All that way along that wall!*
Too far to go.
               I stand smoothing her forehead,
Her child's become her parent, saying with her
The night prayers. She's growing peaceful now.
I'm drawn to the edge of a mystery. The mind
I cannot know, what does it know? She seems

Listening. As a remote landscape listens
To its river in a circle of hills. As a boat
Far out may heed the current beneath,
Bearing it further. What sounds? To us, silence.

Kevin Gilbert
Memorials

Our history is carved
in the heart of the country
our milestone memorials
named Slaughter House Creek
the Coniston massacre, Death
Gully and Durranurrijah
the place on the clifftops called
Massacre Leap,
Evans Head
where the mouth of the valley
filled up with our
murdered dead bodies
the place where our blood flowed
the river ran red
all the way to the sea
At Murramurrang
the land point now baldy
trees withered away
from the sights that they saw
our skeletons lie
in the sand of the beaches
at the base of the cliff
when we could run no more
each skull that we find
is weighed heavy with bullets
the skulls of the children
are crushed and caved in

the cry of the whiteman was:
Slaughter the breeders
wipe out the babies and wipe
out the gins...

Vivian Smith

At an Exhibition of Historical Paintings, Hobart

The sadness in the human visage stares
out of these frames, out of these distant eyes;
the static bodies painted without love
that only lack of talent could disguise.

Those bland receding hills are too remote
where the quaint natives squat with awkward calm.
One carries a kangaroo like a worn toy,
his axe alert with emphasised alarm.

Those nearer woollen hills are now all streets;
even the water in the harbour's changed.
Much is alike and yet a slight precise
disparity seems intended and arranged—

as in that late pink terrace's façade.
How neat the houses look. How clean each brick.
One cannot say they look much older now,
but somehow more themselves, less accurate.

And see the pride in this expansive view:
churches, houses, farms, a prison tower;
a grand gesture like wide-open arms
showing the artist's trust, his clumsy power.

And this much later vision, grander still:
the main street sedate carriages unroll
towards the tentative, uncertain mountain:
a flow of lines the artist can't control—

the foreground nearly breaks out of its frame
the streets end so abruptly in the water...
But how some themes return. A whaling ship.
The last natives. Here that silent slaughter

is really not prefigured or avoided.
One merely sees a profile, a full face,
a body sitting stiffly in a chair:
the soon-forgotten absence of a race...

Album pieces: bowls of brown glazed fruit...
I'm drawn back yet again to those few studies
of native women whose long floral dresses
made them first aware of their own bodies.

History has made artists of all these
painters who lack energy and feature.
But how some gazes cling. Around the hall
the pathos of the past, the human creature.

For My Daughter

Made from nothing: bud and rose,
kisses, water, mystery:
you who grew inside our need
run, in your discovery,

out of the garden's folded light,
out of the green, the fountain's spray,
past the shrubs, the dew-lit ferns,
out to the noise, the street, the day:

and stand, in your astonishment,
beneath the hanging heavy limes
(O my child, O my darling daughter,
summer was full of wars and crimes)

to see the foal, the clown, the doll,
the circus and procession band
march up the street and march away...
And so you turn and take my hand.

Jennifer Strauss
Models

The boys are painting the tanks.
Absorbed, their voices mutter
Terrain, camouflage: 'Not the desert,
Europe.' Delicate,
Respecting brittleness,
The strokes of their brushes
Paint war a game.

Cities have learnt to play it.
Better than ever they rise,
Stone over rubble,
Rubble on bones,
Rotterdam, Dresden, Vienna—
So many phoenixes from Europe's burning.

It's nature
That sometimes sulks,
Throws her hand in—
Fields in the north of France
Grey with an old blight,
Montecassino
Pockmarked in the sun.

Makers of cities
Makers of wars
The boys are playing.
They are painting the tanks.
For more than an hour now
They have not quarrelled.

A Mother's Day Letter: Not for Posting

When you were small you'd fall,
graze a knee, break a collar-bone,
nothing that could not be kissed
and mended—except the blow
death struck, we never spoke of.

I wanted you brave, concerned,
intelligent. Fifteen years late
you tell of fearing your dead
father's anger. What of my pride
that would not consider happiness

in the mere three wishes we get?
Swan-grown you ruffle your plumage
on history's polluted tide.
And I'm like any goose-girl now,
crying 'Come back! Come back!'

'The woods of love are wild
with beasts. In politics' swamp
your sinking feet will hit
toe-breaking boulders of stupidity,
strike razor edges of spite.'

No. Marshal the necessary march.
But if you come back shieldless,
remember I've no appetite for Spartan
deaths. I want you brave,
concerned, intelligent, alive.

Fay Zwicky
From *Four Poems from America*
I   Father in a Mirror

In the morning mirror
you are here in me my eyes
surprised as from our bitter Sundays
cautious, hopeful
silent.

You said, *If it weren't for the Americans...*
while I fought on the other side,
a sullen parody of independence
back in '46.

But Dad, you're here and
I'm the parent now, the shy
explorer taking care and looking
for you at you
in America.

Domestic Architecture

The Wife

A rotary hoist in the front garden
and he's an architect. She's glad
he's rarely home, has even learnt to pardon
a plaster Atlas staggering sad

under a crushing ball among the ferns.
She founders over broken toys,
a rusted cycle in the grass, and yearns
for order. They are childless. It annoys

the neighbours when she nightly sings
    'O neighbours, neighbours, I am growing old.
    My husband built a house and gave me rings.
    The house is dark, my child within grows cold...'

The Architect

She always wanted it, that line.
Against my will I put it in
to please her. Things were fine
till Mum gave us that statue. Always thin,

I couldn't bear the load. I stayed out late,
came home to find her tripping and falling
in grass I couldn't tend. My mate
was heard crying and angrily calling

about some child and a house. We had
no kids. I really don't know why

she made a fuss and it's too bad
to think the neighbours heard the cry...

The Neighbours

We don't know why
our neighbours cry...

Breathing Exercises

Have you ever tried to give your mother breath?

You stand, back to the wall,
a prisoner awaiting execution.

A bad start in life, you might say.
But whose?
We're not talking childbirth.

Desolation keeps you both in check,
as formal as white airless brides.

Her hands undo you, moving in
a slow blind caress,
arching over the clinical sheet
scrunched high in pain.

All you want to do is breathe
the panting mouth alive.
All you want to say, your chances
of being heard saying it,
left the airless room years ago.

Embarrassing scenes in enclosed spaces
were never permitted.

Gagged, you can't move.
Sentence has been passed
without words.

There are no bonds for good behaviour.

Letting Go

Tell the truth of experience
they say they also
say you must let
go learn to let go
let your children
go

and they go
and you stay
letting them go
because you are obedient and
respect everyone's freedom
to go and you stay

and you want to tell the truth
because you are yours truly
its obedient servant
but you can't because
you're feeling what you're not
supposed to feel you have
let them go and go and

you can't say what you feel
because they might read
this poem and feel guilty
and some post-modern hack
will back them up
and make you feel guilty
and stop feeling which is
post-modern and what
you're meant to feel

so you don't write a poem
you line up words in prose

inside a journal trapped
like a scorpion in a locked
drawer to be opened by
your children let go
after lived life and all the time
a great wave bursting
howls and rears and

you have to let go
or you're gone you're
gone gasping you
let go
till the next wave
towers crumbles
shreds you to lace—

When you wake
your spine is twisted
like a sea-bird
inspecting the sky,
stripped by lightning.

David Malouf
The Year of the Foxes
FOR DON ANDERSON

When I was ten, my mother, having sold
her old fox-fur (a ginger red, bone-jawed
Magda Lupescu
of a fox that on her arm played
dead, cunningly dangled
a lean and tufted paw)

decided there was money to be made
from foxes, and bought via
the columns of the *Courier Mail* a whole
pack of them; they hung from penny hooks
in our panelled sitting-room, trailed from the backs

of chairs; and Brisbane ladies, rather
the worse for war, drove up in taxis wearing
a G.I. on their arm
and rang at our front door.

I slept across the hall, at night hearing
their thin cold cry. I dreamed the dangerous spark
of their eyes, brushes aflame
in our fur-hung, nomadic
tent in the suburbs, the dark fox-stink of them
cornered in their holes
and turning…

        Among my mother's show pieces—
Noritaki teacups, tall hock-glasses
with stems like barley-sugar,
goldleaf demitasses—
the foxes, row upon row, thin-nosed, prick-eared,
dead.

     The cry of hounds
was lost behind mirror-glass,
where ladies with silken snoods and finger-nails
of chinese lacquer red
fastened a limp paw;
went down in their high heels
to the warm soft bitumen, wearing at throat
and elbow the rare spoils
of '44: old foxes, rusty-red like dried-up wounds,
and a G.I. escort.

Margaret Scott
Settlers' Graveyard

None of these gaunt stones was raised to an old man,
And most stand over narrow graves like cribs.
One granite pillar, gritting texts like teeth
In the south wind, records the deaths of Karl and Anna Möller,

Parents to a long graven register of beloveds.
In this bleak dormitory where only the grass whispers
They laid to rest eleven sons and daughters
Knowing them in the sacrament of absence.
A towering, ragged land. Here a mother could run
Madder than Lear with a skeletal fool for comfort
Mouthing night and clacking along behind her.
But the migrant woman, tying on laundered aprons,
Stirred ritual possets, laid on poultices,
Closed the eyes and prayed; dressed in her crackling blacks
And trailed the coffins in their long procession
Out to this dour hill. Like Pyrrha she swept home
From the harsh field where the stones trembled to life
In her steady vision: the homes, the river, the valley,
The seas she'd crossed, all distant homelands
Seared in a fiery shroud of amazing trumpets;
And her children, the chosen, rising elect and whole,
Spurning the splitting stone and the shrieking wicked,
Coming in joy for their last long Bible story,
And garnered warm and white within her arms.
Almost the apocalyptic murmur of these bones
Cries pity for the cold earth, the unrepentant waste.

From *Housework*

1   Making Redcurrant Jelly

FOR BEVERLEY FARMER

Today I made redcurrant jelly,
lugging a pan of juice as thick and dark as
water dyed by my grandmother's heavy curtains.
And the face I found in my white enamel well,
looking up from a crimson mirror, was hers to the life
when she bent to knead a trough of steaming rep.
There were her plump cheeks split by shadows,
a glint of spectacles, her horns and wisps of hair.
When I was young she used to tell us stories
of mirrors that spoke in riddles, miraculous wells,

innocent victims of magic, great survivors,
but her eyes that are also mine discouraged questions.
What made the daughter run with her jar to the spring
or the mother carry soup for a stranger god?
As I stirred in sugar the sealed face dissolved
in a swirl of baffling mothers, importunate girls,
labouring since the time that pots were fired
to draw reflecting water from the earth,
to scour, steep, launder, rinse, refine,
to mix soup, remedies, ale, lye, preserves,
recreating always the same image:
vessels of dark fluid, women tied by blood,
brewing, pouring knowledge that goes beyond them.

Chris Wallace-Crabbe
An Elegy

Everything turns out more terrible
than they had said, or what I thought
at midnight they had said,

but the dark marks
tracking across clean snow
way down there must be people,

that is
if anything on earth can be human
when eighteen storeys below,

so that I wish again
it were possible to pluck my son
out of dawn's moist air

by the pylon-legs
in that dewy-green slurred valley
before he ever hit the ground,

to sweep under his plunge
like a pink-tinged angel
and gather him gasping back into this life.

The Inheritance

Dunked into life, a squalling brat
apeing the role of perfect child,
I let this language buoy me up,
shock troops lightly graduated:
nasty, nice, nectarine, nasturtium, noun.

The stuff was rich as mother's milk.
I couldn't see it didn't fit,
making it do so anyway,
eliding what was grossly wrong.
Origins prove nothing, said William James.

I romped round discourse in my room
only devouring foreign books—
northern, that is—containing heath,
lorries, wolves, bobbies and snow.
The signified was quite inadequate,

a mere Australia. City fathers
had long conspired with Empirespeak
by cancelling native foliage;
so every winter English buds
flashed into fluffy pastel bloom again.

As cunning as a leaning dunny,
this international currency
parades its virtue in old rhymes,
tomb after tomb, as death with breath.
We swim along with it. We swim and drown.

Trace Elements

…but surely the dead must walk again.
They stroll most oddly in and out of
small corners of your being, optical blips.
They go with an awkward gait, like foreign changelings
through the edges of a crowd or down the block.

It is at random seasons when the mind
is full at ease that my father, roundshouldered,
shuffles along to wait for lights to change
or my tall son shambles down the footpath
in a woollen cap, relentlessly unfashionable
and quiet as a cloud.
                              What do they want?
Can they be translated?

Space-time is no longer their medium;
                                        they inhabit
antipodes of the radiant fair dinkum,
post-Heisenberg, transphysical, post-Planck,
taunting us all with quips of antimatter.
They are black holes punched in the modern world.
They have been resurrection.
                              They are Dreaming
and we the dream they paint their names across
in grey and lavender and thunderblue,
photocopies of Krishna passing
by Lasseter's reef; or somebody
behind us on the back road to Emmaus,
footsteps in the dust.
                              I would not have it
any other way.
              They walk on by.

Antigone Kefala
Deserted Wife

In black. Made of milk,
warmth of children, toys,
baskets of newly washed clothes,
sunshine, and a skin of
translucent dragonfly wings.

Living in abandoned houses,
afraid of the dark, of the past,
her guileless arms fluttering awkwardly
as those of school girls,
waving good-bye in empty country roads.

Mal Morgan
Arthur Mee

Arthur Mee knew everything
wrote ten encyclopaedias.
He revealed more
than the ten commandments.
His leather-bound red volumes
filled my time
between school, violin
                and radio.

Pages became a magic lantern show.

They turned themselves
from light to dark.

It was the darker side of knowledge
I was after
behind a door
that was always closed
where my father
made love
           to my mother.

Tom Shapcott
From *Instructions for Moving*
XIV   Black Cat

1.   This is an elegy for black cat.

2.   Black cat walked into our kitchen in 1968.
     Black cat died in 1984. She was older
     than all of us. She occupied a place.

3. Black cat, not long after she swept her tail
   and came into her own, gave birth
   to two kittens. She ate each of them.
   She licked herself clean.

4. Black cat had sharp claws and she used them.
   Black cat found a place in the kitchen
   because she was now part of the household.
   We remodeled and she took over
   the narrowest space. She could strike from there.
   Bare legs, children's thighs,
   unsuspecting visitors.

5. I cannot remember if we had black cat spayed.
   I think we did, but she
   would not acknowledge that.

6. Black cat was an urban terrorist.

7. Once, perhaps every six weeks or seven
   black cat would permit one of us to fondle her.
   When she rubbed herself against you
   it was quite specific—
   'Remarkable', we all said. 'Remarkable.'

8. Once black cat was not quick enough.
   In the renovated kitchen with its spring-taut door
   black cat followed me in but her tail was caught.
   Her tail developed a droop. After six weeks
   the dead half fell off.

9. The family divided.
   They say cats cannot move house
   but black cat defined her new territory
   by pissing in each corner.

10. I was in the house (which was now not my own)
    when black cat died.
    She pissed in the bedrooms
    she asked incessantly for sympathy,

ears torn, head huge, tick-scarred, toothless,
her half-tail all dull. Black cat told us
the last tales of her ownership—
how she united things, how we used her
to bind and divide, how she consumed
all of us and all our offerings.
Black cat stretched one paw,
contracted.
What was the old anger, the eating of children?
We have grown separate and intelligent.
Claws reach out—are they teasing?
Old animals have this power.

11. This is an elegy for one black cat.
That cat was never friendly.

12. This elegy is written under duress.
Black cat showed us. More than any animal of ours
the death of black cat claws at our exposed parts.
Her dying was slow we were not sure,
we were dry eyed.
Black cat intended it would be that way.
Our children are the children of black cat.
Now she commands from me this homage.

Ripe Bananas

Do you remember when you first tasted banana?
My childhood was the sub-tropics, banana trees,
mangoes, pawpaws in every backyard, pineapples
in rows, passionfruit over the fence
and the Queensland nut tree across the road
waiting to be raided. Fresh fruit
was home-grown, and in its own season
(though the greengrocer cultivated us with apples,
stone fruit and citrus, he even came to the back door
every Tuesday). Fruit was what you picked yourself
or, like the bananas, it became the full ceremony:
when the bunch showed its first sign of yellowing

the whole tree had to be chopped down.
I still remember the splash of sap and the fibrous trunk
which might be thought truly phallic.
Then the wrist of the fruit-stalk would be severed.
On a good crop there might be seven or eight 'hands'.
We dragged and hoisted the drooping pinnacle under the house
and roped it to the rafters. Its base tailed off
into the last leathery petals, still blood-purple
and folded inward so that even in a family of boys
they looked sensuous, seriously female.
The tree itself had to be shredded and sacrificed,
seasonal king surrounded by the suckering new plants.
And in the dark of the sheltered storage space
each morning we could test and try, after feeding the chooks,
until the first banana was ready. If there were twins,
joined fruit, these were always reserved for me and my brother.

Judith Rodriguez
Eskimo Occasion

I am in my Eskimo-hunting-song mood,
Aha!
The lawn is tundra   the car will not start
the sunlight is an avalanche   we are avalanche-struck at our
    breakfast
struck with sunlight through glass   me and my spoonfed
    daughters
out of this world in our kitchen.

I will sing the song of my daughter-hunting,
Oho!
The waves lay down   the ice grew strong
I sang the song   of dark water under ice
the song of winter fishing   the magic for seal rising
among the ancestor-masks.

I waited by water to dream new spirits,
Hoo!

The water spoke   the ice shouted
the sea opened   the sun made young shadows
they breathed my breathing   I took them from deep water
I brought them fur-warmed home.

I am dancing the years of the two great hunts,
Ya-hay!
It was I who waited   cold in the wind-break
I stamp like the bear   I call like the wind of the thaw
I leap like the sea spring-running. My sunstruck daughters
    splutter
and chuckle and bang their spoons:

Mummy is singing at breakfast and dancing!
So big!

An Upbringing

I have come home to you and mudcrab.
Never inclined to put off, to keep expectation polished,
always a gulper and gobbler for present titbits,
a gabbler they slowed over years of rebukes and debating,
I am learning now what presenters kept dinning in vain:
there's a thing I have starved half a lifetime for, ignorantly.
A word for it, my preferred and penultimate term for it—
    mudcrab.

All my childhood the high mystery of mudcrab
—charred Rousseau angel, volant, with French horn—
hung above Sunday early, the way to the Broadwater.
We'd be putting away single peanuts, sighting
milestones in the left-hand grass. Dad knew them all.
At this creek, or was it the other, there'd be talk
of yabbying, shadowy mangroves to seaward, and mudbanks
of the legendary and incomparable mudcrab,
denizen of sucking shallows and dark silt tideflats.
And what hints of the wild-man guile of the getters of
    mudcrab!

Ritual meat, it was not for children or tennis-friends.
It was laid in, by the ritual half-dozen, for Big Boss from
    Stockholm,
who missed out on two lots—six swelling the boot of the
    Holden
and six in containers, pinched for space, in the fridge.
In the end, containers and all, mudcrab rose
apocalyptic on mornings of heat
to rout us from house and car and land, appalled.
Mum swung the door, Dad ran with Courier'd mudcrab
stretched five-arms'-length off, later hosed the boot,
and we closed every single back window tight for cloudless
    days
before trying to do something with the bin. The curse of
    mudcrab.

So misguidedly, on a birthday shout at Lennons',
parents' friend footing the bill, I flouted for foreigners
the homeshore mudcrab. On from caviar—Dad demurred—
to Bombe Alaska in its chocolate carapace, cocking
a green-toffee butterfly, roaming crimson jelly,
spilling its Sundae guts of fruit-salad and ice-cream.
The great mudcrab shrugged his shell and went back down
    his hole.

Growing up. One way of putting it: dodging mudcrab.
The years of 'austerity' when the Best was desperately
    still-and-always
British, for pleasure read principle, the luxury of high art
held for questioning, a migrant with un-Australian habits.
And mudcrab was hiding out in the creeks down the bay.

Cordelia's Music for Lear

If I tell you your liegemen wait
and your monster horse
you peer through the crazed hedge
show off bird-tufts

and paste them with licky
to a horse-skull melting like candy.
You have to laugh.

Come from the twigs, summon
the lineage of straw
colouring-in our blood
to daub your scratches.
Father, I gather
your warrior-hand all bone
in my hand's bowl,

in my shawl, in my hair's shade.
My young esquires
paint birds on their shields
each golden eye
and rainy bird-voice
a washed soul beginning.
Lie soft, be called.

Les Murray
Evening Alone at Bunyah

1

My father, widowed, fifty-six years old,
sits washing his feet.
The innocent sly charm
is back in his eye of late years, and tonight
he's going dancing.

I wouldn't go tonight, he says to me
by way of apology. *You sure you won't come?*
What for? I ask. *You know I only dance
on bits of paper.* He nods and says, *Well, if
any ghosts come calling, don't let 'em eat my cake.*

I bring him a towel and study his feet afresh:
they make my own feel coarse. They are so small,

so delicate he can scarcely bear to walk
barefoot to his room to find his dancing shoes
and yet all day he works in hobnailed boots
out in the forest, clearing New South Wales.

No ghosts will come, Dad. I know you dote on cake.
I know how some women who bake it dote on you.
It gets them nowhere.
You are married still.

2

Home again from the cities of the world.
Cool night, and the valley relaxes after heat,
the earth contracts, the planks of the old house creak,
making one more adjustment, joist to nail,
nail to roof, roof to the touch of dew.

Smoke stains, rafters, whitewash rubbed off planks...
yet this is one house that Jerry built to last:
when windstorms came, and other houses lost
roofs and verandahs, this gave just enough
and went unscathed, for all the little rain
that sifted through cracks, the lamps puffed out by wind
sucked over the wallplate, and the occasional bat
silly with fear at having misplaced the dark.

When I was a child, my father was ashamed
of this shabby house. It signified for him
hard work and unjust poverty. There would come
a day when he'd tear it down and build afresh.
The day never came. But that's another poem.

No shame I felt in those days was my own.
It can be enough to read books and camp in a house.
Enough, at fourteen, to watch your father sit
at the breakfast table nursing his twelve-gauge
shotgun, awaiting the doubtful reappearance
of a snake's head at a crack in the cement
of the skillion fireplace floor.

The blood's been sluiced
away, and the long wrecked body of the snake
dug out and gone to ash these thirteen years,
but the crack's still there,
and the scores the buckshot ripped beside the stove.

3

There is a glow in the kitchen window now
that was not there in the old days. They have set
three streetlights up along the Gloucester road
for cows to stray by, and night birds to shun,
for the road itself's not paved, and there's no town
in the valley yet at all.
It is hoped there will be.

Today, out walking, I considered stones.
It used to be said that I must know each one
on the road by its first name, I was such a dawdler,
such a head-down starer.
I picked up
a chunk of milk-seamed quartz, thumbed off the clay,
let the dry light pervade it and collect,
eliciting shifting gleams, revealing how
the specific strength of a stone fits utterly
into its form and yet reflects the grain
and tendency of the mother-lode, the mass
of a vanished rock-sill tipping one small stone
slightly askew as it weighs upon your palm,
and then I threw it back towards the sun
to thump down on a knoll
where it may move a foot in a thousand years.

Today, having come back, summer was all mirror
tormenting me. I fled down cattle tracks
chest-deep in the earth, and pushed in under twigs
to sit by cool water speeding over rims
of blackened basalt, the tall light reaching me.

Since those moth-grimed streetlamps came,
my dark is threatened.

4

I stand, and turn, and wander through the house,
avoiding those floorboards that I know would creak,
to the other verandah. Here is where I slept,
and here is where, one staring day, I felt
a presence at my back, and whirled in fright
to face my father's suit, hung out to air.

This country is my mind. I lift my face
and count my hills, and linger over one:
Deer's, steep, bare-topped, where eagles nest below
the summit in scrub oaks, and where I take
my city friends to tempt them with my past.

Across the creek and the paddocks of the moon
four perfect firs stand dark beside a field
lost long ago, which holds a map of rooms.
This was the plot from which we transplants sprang.
The trees grew straight. We burgeoned and spread far.
I think of doors and rooms beneath the ground,
deep rabbit rooms, thin candlelight of days...
and, turning quickly, walk back through the house.

5

Night, and I watch the moonrise through the door.
Sitting alone's a habit of mind with me...
for which I'll pay in full. That has begun.
But meanwhile I will sit and watch the moon.

My father will be there now, at a hall
in the dark of the country, shining at the waltz,
spry and stately, twirling at formal speeds
on a roaring waxed-plank floor.

The petrol lamps
sizzle and glare now the clapping has died down.
They announce some modern dance. He steps outside
to where cigarettes glow sparsely in the dark,
joins some old friends and yarns about his son.

Beneath this moon, an ancient radiance comes
back from far hillsides where the tall pale trunks
of ringbarked trees haphazardly define
the edge of dark country I could not afford
to walk in at night alone
lest I should hear
the barking of dogs from a clearing where no house
has ever stood, and, walking down a road
in the wilderness, meet a man who waited there
beside a creek to tell me what I sought.

Father, come home soon.
Come home alive.

The Mitchells

I am seeing this: two men are sitting on a pole
they have dug a hole for and will, after dinner, raise
I think for wires. Water boils in a prune tin.
Bees hum their shift in unthinning mists of white

bursaria blossom, under the noon of wattles.
The men eat big meat sandwiches out of a styrofoam
box with a handle. One is overheard saying:
drought that year. Yes. Like trying to farm the road.

The first man, if asked, would say *I'm one of the Mitchells.*
The other would gaze for a while, dried leaves in his palm,
and looking up, with pain and subtle amusement,

say *I'm one of the Mitchells.* Of the pair, one has been rich
but never stopped wearing his oil-stained felt hat. Nearly
    everything
they say is ritual. Sometimes the scene is an avenue.

Home Suite

Home is the first
and final poem
and every poem between
has this mum home seam.

Home's the weakest enemy
as iron steams starch—
but to war against home
is the longest march.

Home has no neighbours.
They are less strong
than the tree, or the sideboard.
All who come back belong.

Home is the contraband
alike of rubble squats
and of where food is never
cooked in the old death fats:

Can you fuse a new joint
home in this circuit-tier?
Does each trail a long home
to fold and unfurl here?

Streets of bulldozed terrace
or that country of the Shark,
or with slant cattle-launching
ramps adzed from ironbark—

All soft invisible flag-days
fawn pasts sting with pride:
the world's oldest lamplight
stumbles from inside

as I come to the door
and they're all there
in Serbia, Suburbia,
in the chill autumn air.

No later first-class plane
flies the sad quilt wings.
Any feeling after final
must be home, with idyll-things.

First home as last
is a rounded way to live
but to tell another You're my home
speaks of a greater love.

Love. It is a recent
and liquid enough term
to penetrate and mollify
what's compact in home.

Ian Templeman
My Father's Letter

This father, my father, as father and son am I,
has found his voice, sings in his eighty-sixth year.
He stretches in the growing dark. No longer shy
of words he begins to dismantle the lifelong fear

of language, delighted with a newly found power
to assemble images. He speaks through rambling
family letters, recording the detail of his day, hour
by hour, exploring the page in spare, gambolling

script without concern for syntax, punctuation.
Breaking my mother's double act, in solo performance,
he curses, expresses regret at my expatriation,
confesses a dreaminess, reveals unexpected eloquence.

I am to my child as my father is to me, my heart dumb;
mute stranger until I hear the rattle of death's drum.

Mudrooroo
Song One

Jacky's features worn and craggy,
The face of the cliff behind his place,
Worn and fissured with the care of his race,
Seeing them come and seeing them go,
Bodies bent or straight, weak or strong—
Seeing them go and wanting to follow,
First, he must fix his self and his self:
Jacky's not one to forget, remembering too much,
Remembers it all and wants to know more,
Wants to forget wages of flour, sugar and tea,
Wages of flour, sugar and tea, and women bought for a drink.

Jacky sits under the sun, feeling the warmth so good,
Feeling himself lying back, reclining with his head in his hands,
Reclining and thinking drowsily in the shade.
Peaceful his body, restless his mind,
Father tall and strong and fretful,
Circumcised into the Rain Dream, born from the Lizard,
Cast out at a little place, on a table in a shed,
Near a town, a whiteman's town, not too good or bad for
    Kooris.

Jacky lying back, body resting, mind, it roams,
Riding a wind, holding on and recalling—
His wife, a lissom girl with a tongue as quick as her wit.
Met her in some other place and took her back
To his shack, now a house, where she does what she does.
Of the Frog Dream mated with the Dog,
Woman rounded of breasts and thighs,
Rounded and a mother of two boys and girls.

Two boys, the eldest ran the store;
Followed the old ways and had been made a man;
Other still in school, beard beginning to show,
Just the other day copped for underage drinking.
Eldest daughter, sixteen married herself to a man
He did not like, one who wore suits and spoke with a lisp,
Collected a salary, now she was pregnant and lived in the town.

Mind restless, mind roaming this way and that,
Daughter, a baby herself, now a mother too soon—
Well, that was life, and when was the last time he had gone
Hunting for a 'roo or even a cow, rabbits don't count,
He thought as he lay, while the sun
Made a run up the sky and fell over
In a blazing circle of thunderclaps ripping the earth,
And wrenching from the craggy cliff-face
A boulder beginning to fall,
Crashing down and rolling along to Jacky,
Picking him up and taking him home to tea and scones.

J.S. Harry
After the Money for the Milk

After the money for the milk—
light fingers, light feet—
but the bottles
        clinked on the step;
we turned on the light
to catch the thief—

    We did not
            find out
what you wanted with it,
son, not yet six...
most children
            steal a little   I did not
beat you, though there was
some-talk-of-it—and an

irrational sense of disgrace,
you died   before
we grew over it;   it grows over you,
my disgrace.

But the earth
weighs heavier   colder upon you, may it not
press, may you not feel, this earth,
my weight.

Mousepoem

Her lover departed
to the warm purry
bed of his wife,
with pale blue hands
in the cold dawnlight
she has written a poem so slight
she thinks if a mouse breathed on it,
it would collapse (the
poem, not

        the mouse which is made
of tough, mouse material, whiskers, ears,
small, quick, risk-assessing eyes; the poem
is so light it seems to float, not stand;
the mouse…stands on firm mouse-muscles
& potato-crispy, cat-delighting
bones.) Who would ever think of fucking
a mouse, but its lover? Who would ever
want to be fucked by a mouse but another?
Who would wish for blind, hairless
mouse-children, but a mousy mother?
Does a mouse wish
or are children merely what happens to it
wishless but wanting?
Time: is a moment
a mouse at rest? Pick it up? You cannot.
Relativity (by neither Newton's nor Einstein's

mechanics): when a human moves
a live mouse refuses arrest.
Even a blind mouse
will feel the great weight
of a malnutritioned
skinny human
& dart for the soot-stinky hole
behind a dead fire's
cold grate.

What has her slight poem
to do with a dead fire?
                                    Ah…

Aileen Kelly
My Brother's Piano

Sigmund Freud's sister, a promising concert pianist, was limited
to practising on a silenced piano so as not to disturb his study and
writing.

In the darkened library
I find my brother's piano
and with his own well-stropped razor
cut the two (in my dream clearly)
essential strings
not to stop him playing
I think
but to keep distraction under control.
Awake I recognise it is not so simple.

*

He makes a sad exhibit acting out
his pathological diversion
in the natural domain of women:
accomplishments to decorate
their domesticity and the lives of families
with elegance and art.

If I were to write in real day
the book I assemble nightly
in the darkened library
his drive would be described as piano envy.

*

For five precious hours tonight
as he was playing at the concert hall
the house was silent of the boom and trill
that break ideas into distraction.
I was not at my desk no
a sister's place is in the audience.
I made a few useful observations
of couple interaction among the various
strata of the crowd but was aware
all evening of my room
its pool of quiet
where I could not bathe.

*

Young men talk to me
endlessly of themselves. It is so
easy to remember and analyse.
I have compiled (despite the boom the trill
the emotional self-aggrandisement)
several hundred envelopes of notes
cross-referenced,
the synthesis begins.
In real day I cannot enter
much that is relevant of the libraries
for fear of shocking the male scholars.
I am no longer shocked by my own mind
but understand
if I write in real day the book
I assemble nightly in the darkened library
the author's name must seem masculine.

*

Last night
in the darkened library
with my bare shining hands
I twisted the three pedals
from my brother's piano
thinking That will silence him
him and his fugues.
There will be a chapter on such dreams.

Geoffrey Lehmann
From *Pieces for My Father*

IV

On his sore ageing legs my father rubs
Rose embrocation from an old brown bottle,
And the hot dusk and sticky scent bring back
Childhood vacations, warm nights, citronella,
Queensland and steam trains crawling over bridges
And jerking us past moonlit canefields,
A cat leaping at brown-cream butterflies,
My sunburned legs itching from sandfly scabs,
My father laughing as I run from wasps
And photographing island scenes and us
Swimming in waves like shimmering insect wings.
Rose embrocation and its swarming scent,
And I would hold my father here against
The window blue with dusk for ever.
Night folds us in and stings us with her stars.

The Flight of Children

On Friday afternoons and back on Sunday
routinely strapping themselves in, they fly
each week or fortnight, unaccompanied
except for teddy, digital watch or headset.

Snow splashed on mountain ranges, cumulus
at sunset puffed in sumo wrestling poses
are as familiar as the stippled lines
of rain that race across the perspex porthole,

repetitive as the safety demonstrations,
the juice and biscuit balanced on a tray.
Always there is a room, which is their own,
with battered animals, where they can't be,

a parent they must leave, to see the other.
They dream of moving cities by some act
of childish will. Maps, coastlines are transformed
and two rooms are a skateboard ride apart.

'Menindee'

At thirty-three my brother-in-law
is dying
of a hatband that chafed a mole.
With seven children—
three his own,
four others the children of a dead man—
he won't give in.
Married at last to the woman he battled for,
still begetting children,
after the brandmark showed,
he insists that unwilling surgeons
cut as each secondary appears;
excoriated and scarred
in a one-man cosmic war
against death.
In the last year he has built a dam,
purchased a capacious deep freeze,
set the fences in order
and the women are saying their prayers.
My sister is in a state of collapse.
This year with spring
cruelly lush and wet

his false lucerne tree flowered profusely.
The lilac he planted,
and other costly trees and shrubs
are just coming on,
but my sister, the horse rider,
is a ghost of her beauty,
lined and haggard with his war.
The children she knitted and sewed for
are growing unkempt like weeds,
and the house
the cream wooden cottage on the flat
tucked away in an elbow of creek
among pepper trees and haystacks
is an empty shell hole
where they subsist
in the lushest summer for years.

There are spiders on the fibro veranda
and cats germinating under the boards.
Clothes are scattered on the laundry floor.
Two summers ago newly married
they would lie there, idly joking,
soaking up coolness from the concrete slab,
gazing at the ceiling, dim green
from the garden's glare.

This is chronic country,
terminal perhaps for some.
After ten years of drought and waiting,
the lush seasons have come
and wool has collapsed—

Terminal for the big establishments
with big mortgages
building up their flocks for years
and borrowing, and now
they're selling prize rams for carcases.

We are sheep farmers
and nobody wants us—
driving at night through paddocks
the eyes of sheep in our headlights
are green incandescent jelly,
shaking and moving away as our tyres bite through gravel.
Men reject the soft wool
which comforted us in the Ark,
preferring the loveless synthetics,
false economics.
But beware, your children
will curse you for letting dodoes die,
half of the natural world perish,
and when our flocks have dwindled
you may not entice us back.

This planet which tries to house
half of the men who have ever lived
wants no one in particular.
It does not want you, either—

We are all sheep farmers.

Myself I wage no cosmic wars,
I travel light
with my five hundred acres,
half of it uncleared, kangaroo country
because no one wants
what it would grow.
With my bees and yellow jonquils
and journeys with a carload of calves,
trading in a small way,
I survive.

My sister still desperately beautiful
rides the boundaries of their big establishment.
One of her children sleeps with his eyes open.

Kate Llewellyn
Divorce

Before I told my children
their father was leaving
to live with his mistress,
I read three books on the topic
to see how it was done.

After that news
they went on eating their chops.
Amazed, I could see the books were right—
if you're calm, they will be.

Yet the boy said, 'But we'll be lonely'.
'No, we won't', I said,
'he'll come and visit us
and you'll visit them'.

And that's how quietly, hopefully
and gently World War III began.

Jan Owen
Freud and the Vacuum Cleaner

It comes of reading psychology late at night
for insomnia. I should have tried milk instead
of two learned neo-Freudians who categorically state
my cleaner's a phallic symbol extraordinaire.
Now six in ten years is a high mortality rate
for symbols: the implications are clear.
Yet I dutifully read the manuals
and used the attachments with care;
cruised with the purring Lark over the Wilton's greyish-white
till the day it choked on a sock and some knickers (not mine);
I gently restrained the GE as it mounted the mat—
it was shorted by a size three screw, not me;

and that Spanish one with the rattle was crook from the start.
Even the ones I had on loan went back with a wheeze
or their rubbers half off.
My husband says enough is enough,
four times a week will wear the carpet out.
'I'm only obeying the Makers' Instructions,' I hiss,
'they're simply not made to last.'
On Thursday, the latest, still quite new,
a National (recommended by *Choice*),
lost a knob, slipped its roller, went flaccid,
stopped sucking and blew.
And of course I'd misplaced the guarantee.
Still, I've gained some relief from the *Saturday Review*
(The *Age*, February 23, 1985)
where all things Freudian are cast in doubt
by Dr Jeffrey Masson of Berkeley, U.S.A.
who has found the truth
in a big black box near Anna's bed:
a thousand suppressed letters—
a case of fraud he claims.
And now the Doktor's built-in obsolescence comes to light
I'm quite absolved of blame—
I'm not a castrating woman, not a polymorphic pervert—
a household appliance simply takes less time
to wear out than a household name.
So 'What does a woman really want?'
The answer is not an upright.
My newest replacement is the cylinder sort,
a tubby trundling pet on a trachea leash.
I'm playing it safe, there's nothing suspect about that,
although, as the sales-girl pointed out,
if it's got the wattage, it's got the power,
and this one's appetite lifts the carpet off the floor.
It was only after I signed the cheque, I swear,
I read, in plastic letters of gold across the maroon,
Conquest 1000, my new model's name.

Geoff Page
My Mother's God

My mother's God
has written the best
of the protestant proverbs:

you make the bed
you lie in it;
God helps him

who helps himself.
He tends to shy away from churches,
is more to be found in

phone calls to daughters
or rain clouds over rusty grass.
The Catholics

have got him wrong entirely:
too much waving the arms about,
the incense and caftan, that rainbow light.

He's leaner than that,
lean as a pair of
grocer's scales,

hard as a hammer at cattle sales
the third and final
time of asking.

His face is most clear
in a scrubbed wooden table
or deep in the shine of a

laminex bench.
He's also observed at weddings and funerals
by strict invitation, not knowing quite

which side to sit on.
His second book, my mother says,
is often now too well received;

the first is where the centre is,
tooth for claw and eye for tooth
whoever tried the other cheek?

Well, Christ maybe,
but that's another story.
God, like her, by dint of coursework

has a further degree in predestination.
Immortal, omniscient, no doubt of that,
he nevertheless keeps regular hours

and wipes his feet clean on the mat,
is not to be seen at three in the morning.
His portrait done in a vigorous charcoal

is fixed on the inner
curve of her forehead.
Omnipotent there

in broad black strokes
he does not move.
It is not easy, she'd confess,

to be my mother's God.

Middle Names

Middle names
are where the distaff
surfaces
and disappears;
your mother's father's
name is carried
one bend further
down the years.
The middle name
becomes a talisman;
superstition
keeps it on;
a polished stone

inside a pocket
thrown out when the
owner's gone
or carried through
as secret totem,
not quite knowing
what it meant,
a river, town or
English shire,
some misty village
lost in Kent.
Ambition, with its
sterner stuff,
reads further on
along the line.
Ted, or Tom,
gives way to Tarquin,
more suited to that
vast design.
A few are heirs
to three or four,
a forest thick
with family trees,
and catch perhaps
some withered branches
rattling thinly
in the breeze.
Middle names
go deeper down,
always the obverse
of the coin—
and hesitate
like kids at parties,
waiting to be

asked to join.
Or choose to plume
themselves a little.
Freed from the gospels'
narrow choices,
they listen to
obscure ambitions,
the vanity in
buried voices.
Americans
use pure initials;
they have no centre
to confess.
The man who author-
ised the Bomb
is known as only
'Harry S.'
The middle name's
another self,
the cleric's daring
libertine,
the hedonist
on Sunday evening
washing socks
and conscience clean.

The middle name's
another person,
that happier
alternative,
the person who
we might have been,
someone easier
to forgive.

Craig Powell
It Used to be Different

'I am distressed for thee, my brother Johnathan.
Very pleasant hast thou been to me.
Thy love for me was wonderful,
passing the love of women.'

You've changed toward me since you found a wife.
I sit at home here every night and wonder,
'Why doesn't he ring?'
                                   But you don't ring.
So I get drunk and punch my wife across
the face and it's your fault.

It used to be different. I was important to you.
In Glebe you were sitting at the bus stop when
you saw me coming. I'd been away in Brisbane.
But you ran toward me and hugged me like a brother
and said, 'Come and have dinner with me! Buy
a few bottles!' You were so glad I was back.
It meant everything.

                        Lovely girl, your wife.

Oh God, you bloody fool, no wonder I'm drunk!
I want to punch everything! I love you more
than my own brother. You sit there full of yourself
and your good life and you never understand
there was something between us.
                                   Now you're tired of me.
You've got other friends, I suppose, and of course you're married.
It doesn't matter.
                        Christ I'm drunk tonight!

Is it getting late?
                        Time for you to go home.
No. Don't stay if you don't want to. Good night.
Yes, Yes, it was nice seeing you again.

It was nice.
And keep in touch.
                    I'll wait for you to ring.

Andrew Taylor
The Dead Father

Rainy wind's banging the back gate
open to the street
where neighbours shelter behind verandas—
though a shadow of blue sky
claims this is only a shower
and will pass over like the day itself

Inside it's warm and the kitchen smells
toasty and full of 3YB and coffee
my father's on holiday
we'll go for a picnic and light a fire for chops
and watch his spirit spiral toward heaven
through the dripping trees

My lemon tree
unburdened at last of its fruit
stretches and shakes ungovernably in the wind—
why after nine years should his death be here
in a moment of rain and my small garden
blown suddenly open to the street?

                        *

His method of relaxing
was to change from blue business suit
into brown—late in the forties
brown was relaxing, or was it
really that those brown suits hanging thriftily on
since the thirties were only good now
for gardening and our winter
picnics?
            I couldn't tell

who rebelled one summer in the relentless forties
and came to lunch late without a shirt
and was tolerated from then on
aged about eight

*

Considering our picnics were laboriously organised
sequences of semi-disasters—
rain, totally burnt chops, blow-outs
several almost-bushfires—
and I as the youngest whimperingly tired
aching in knees and armpits
boneless and sagged and asleep before home—
why did they bother?
The garden was almost as big as a farm—
I even lost my fourth birthday there
absorbed in my city in a sandpit

Is that why I like this now
my small all-at-a-glance yard
its intricate alleys and stalks
its endless ways of finding myself
in rain and mistily
face to face with him?

*

He was the gentlest person I've known—
hurting him was like hacking with a pick
in a claypan
    I'd do it over and over
until I'd hacked a big O of anguish
in his face and then I'd watch it
close over, swallowing the pain

It was much the same in hospital—
we'd watch the green flicker of his heart
stumble over the screen
while his hand closed on mine

obliterating it in his
just-endurable present

He said he didn't feel any pain
when he died
he'd taken it so far inside
it was only a little more of himself
he had to know and finally
bequeath to us

                              *

He comes back these winter days
as the time he went to Sydney and I stayed
two weeks with his mother, rain falling
like today. In an iron house
she taught me the sound of rain
who had grown up under tile.
I discovered I'd been sleeping deaf
to one of the world's replenishing noises

He's a weather mood
an adjunct of loneliness—
once I went into a dozen bars
'Hey, have you seen my Dad
the one who died ten days ago?'
'Have a drink, son' they'd say
'you might just catch him up
if you don't hurry
So take it easy.'

Jennifer Rankin
Daub Wall

Tonight I am nudged by the fire into another place.
The family pines, silk-screened to an earlier sky
trip me and I know at the bush hut the mason bees
are waiting in wattle and daub walls for the morning.

I have seen them emerge while the air still steamed
with my breath, lying in my child bed, my brother
watching the paddock through the torn verandah blind.

They spend years crawling out of their holes,
dotting the golden sandpaper walls of our hut
until we grow and think of it crumbling, falling
back into the soft yellow dust where we play.

The children are comforted with the pointing out
of time and the slow journey of the striped bees.

At first we were content to trap the creatures
in jam jars with brown perforated paper lids
watching them die outside their meandering holes.
Later we tried a sophisticated spray. It was the fifties.

Our English grandmother's lemon tree continued to bear
although we regularly transplanted the absurd holly.

In our teens we caught greater numbers of bees
always intending to send them away to a government
department or some other place of science, certain
that the damage to the walls could only be marginal.

In summer the mason bees and blowflies mingled
with the kerosene primus and our whistling kettle.

In the middle of the day the paddock grass stood
straight under my mother's blanket and my sister
carried tea trays piled with paperback romance.
Near the verandah the she-oaks reminded me and tonight

I would like to know how the wattle and daub walls have worn.

Poem for David

A small girl draws a circle in the sand.
Inside the circle she places a stone and a stick.
Inside the circle she draws a target.

She turns to us.
She is our daughter.

'Which of these things is most valuable?'
Her voice is high. Questions fall out of the sun.
The sea laps at the circle.
Her feet dance in the sand.

I choose the stone, for endurance.
My son chooses the stick, to catch fish.
Our daughter has chosen the target.

'Because it is mine. I made it myself.'

Margaret Bradstock
Letter to My Daughter
FOR CATHY

The song never did
come out right, did it girl.
The hallucinogenic dream
   out of kilter,
      like a home-movie
         run backwards,
or viewed erratically,
   through a numb haze
of alcohol & dope.
Even then it came unstuck
in the weeks of shots
& passports, sore arms
   & visa cards. It was
someone else's dream, unscaleable,
horizons like glaciers.

We drove you to the airport,
face ripped across with grief
(leaving one boy, & going
   with another),
backpack spilling

travellers cheques & face-lotion,
&, *watch it* we said
　　or you'll find your passport missing
　　　　& your pack full of hash, or worse.
Bangkok to Nepal, perhaps Goa
(the Golden Triangle's
　　an awful bottleneck);
apolitical, you've gone
　　for the clothes & the beaches.
You're frightened of flying
(They've been known to hit
　　the odd mountain)
scared of so many things,
I only just found out.

Are you disappointed in me,
　　you used to ask,
　　　　& I always said no
remembering you in Bali, rowing,
talking Indonesian with the boatman,
　　eyes tracking distant temples.
(The heart's a strange compass,
why do we trust it?)

You phone from Katmandu,
from the smudged glass of a call-box,
　　we can't hear each other.
Love you too, you shout.
　　Now a huge yellow moon is rising
along mountain ranges
& deepcut valleys,
temple bells sound faintly,
　　wind-chimes in the chaos
of an empty room,
& the same old song
is beating in your veins.

Lee Cataldi

northshoredirector'sdaughterweds easternsuburbsdirector'sdaughter

they won't like the news
unable to meet at dinner and congratulate each other
on the merger

    will they see us
    in the new light
    we shine on each other

    no ceremony confirms
    what we do to each other
    but it's real all the same
    real as rain

    is it dangerous
    to go on

    in the darkness of that night
    Freud held up a light
    going down
    into my own bloodstream
    I know I'm not alone

optimism
harsh coals out of horrid experience
remembering
snowstorms
are born in the sun

From *Kuukuu Kardiya and the Women Who Live on the Ground*

2

    the white woman
    comes out of the house she says
        wash the clothes
        finish the job   wipe

the children's noses we are
taking these children away
it's for their own good

the women who live on the ground
disappear into the desert
stepping lightly
out of their regulation mission bloomers
their ragged jumble sale clothing

their voices fade as water
sinks back underground

jukurra jukurra they say
taking their children with them

into the heart of that furnace
where spirits rise whiter than clay

3

the women are in the school
with the children who
are learning to read
yirdi they say
wirlinyirnalu yanu marluku
we went hunting for kangaroo
walyangka karnalu nyina
we live on the ground

the white woman
riding her mop like a broomstick
screams about the building
        what a waste of time   they should be
        learning to spell must and ought
        they are filthy look
        at their noses   look
        at the dust on the floor   look
        at the dust on the ground

outside the school the children
write *warlpiri* in the dust write
kuukuu kardiya in the dust the hot wind
blows into eyes throats noses
into all the clean clothes

the women who live on the ground
watch the white women fade
after a few years
back into their motor cars
after one or two of those seasons in which
the spirits of the secret places
open their giant lungs
and burn the houses to ash

Silvana Gardner
Forbidden Language

One family, yet the grandmother speaks
a foreign language, mother and father
yet another and the daughter another again.

They're not clever for speaking in many tongues!
Sometimes no one understands what the other says
least of all the child who blames wars for sifting
them like sand to countries with no affinities.
Words from other races are seeds implanted
in the lining of their clothes, secret contraband
for the sterility in foreign climates.

The matriarch speaks privately to her son.
He recoils from starched collars in Montenegro
and Greek Orthodox uncles with amethyst rings
for the abstinence of hard liquor and Muslim women.
The child hears Mongol war cries and the ransack
of her sleep. She'll never be taught how to utter
with mouths of Kotor, nor how Turks made love
in times of peace.

Robert Adamson

My First Proper Girlfriend

The first girl I wanted to marry
was Joan Hunter
her father owned more oyster leases
than anyone else on the river

she had buck teeth
but she looked okay really

we'd sit on her father's wharf
and watch the mullet together for hours

they will take over the world one day

we loved each other alright

my parents hated us being together
and called her Bugs Bunny

One night my father cut Joan's Dad
with a fishing knife
right down his left cheek

that little protestant bludger
with his stuck-up bitch of a daughter

Fishing with My Stepson

We wake by your watch on my wrist,
its piercing silicon-chip
alarm, bat-squealing, needling
through our room in The Angler's Rest.
We drink Coke from a plastic Esky
with ice melting into newspaper
wrapped squid, the only
unfrozen bait in town. In perfect dawn
we set out from Don's Boats,
the outboard ploughs us through a bay,
at Juno Point we cast our silver

Tobys, our new Swedish lures,
your pure graphite rod flashes
in first light; your graceful cast
sails out fine as spiderweb,
the smooth water mirrors the arc.
A year passes in the minute it takes
for you to reel in your first true catch,
the rod-bending, line-singing
realizing strike and the flash of fish-fire,
the final buck underwater dash
of a school jewfish, its explosion in air,
and for that split second of communion between us,
utter wonder.

The Australian Crawl

I watched your body fluttering across
the pool, your hands little buckets
chucking water on the flames. The bushfire
was background music as the kids

sploshed about in the wading area.
All this time and we believed our bodies
meant something, life at least.
Birthdays shivered up our spines

sparks in the pallid undergrowth of hair
greying and uncurling. In this dream
our first picnic sails along
on a blanket just above the flames.

The women wearing gingham frocks
making it seem so very sad, Uncle John
juggling his belly on a tricycle.
The bacon-rind on the sliced bread

a wizened hieroglyph meaning nothing,
the cucumber circles sitting on the sockets
of your mother's eyes. Back at home
on the shelf conch-shells

sitting next to books become
little inkwells of nasty beliefs.
The silver we never used dancing
on the table like soft silver tadpoles

sequential meanings drift into meltdown.
The pale-headed rosella a smudge
on the bathroom mirror, the whole house
full of an awful music chuffing

and percussing into your head—
a rat-a-tat and an Australian
threadfin salmon came down south
while you were fishing hookless in the sky.

A picture becomes three-dimensional,
it's Tassie the cat, fleas scooting down
his tail into the fish-tank, outside cockatoos
flurry, inside a Wettex shivers in the sink.

Wendy Poussard
Telegram from Grandmother

PROTEST LADIES
COURT HOUSE
ALICE SPRINGS

STAY TOGETHER REMEMBER WHAT
HAPPENED TO THE WALLS OF JERICHO
                    BEST WISHES
                    GRANDMOTHER

One of the many messages of support received by women at Pine
Gap during the Peace Camp in November 1983.

Dear Grandmother

Thank you for your encouragement
and good advice.
You may be interested to hear
that since your telegram arrived

we have, with songs and drums,
and a handy pair of bolt-cutters
actually breached the walls
or more precisely fence
and taken down the gates,
a cause of some embarrassment
to the men of Jericho.

The sun, while not exactly still,
takes a slow walk
across our works and days.
I keep my hat on
and freckle slowly.

Having survived so well
in all your years
you put the first things first.
The getting down
of walls and fences is the easy part.
Here in the dust
to stay together
is what tears the heart.
We change a little day by day
so that it may be possible
to tell our daughters' daughters
'stay together'.

Grandmother keep us always in your prayers.

John Tranter
Backyard

The God of Smoke listens idly in the heat
  to the barbecue sausages
speaking the language of rain deceitfully
  as their fat dances.

Azure, hazed, the huge drifting sky shelters
  its threatening weather.

A screen door slams, and the kids come tumbling
    out of their arguments,

and the barrage of shouting begins, concerning
    young Sandra and Scott
and the broken badminton racquet and net
    and the burning meat.

Is that a fifties home movie, or the real
    thing? Heavens, how
a child and a beach ball in natural colour
    can break your heart.

And the brown dog worries the khaki grass
    to stop it from growing
in place of his worship, the burying bone.
    The bone that stinks.

Turn now to the God of this tattered arena
    watching over the rites
of passage—marriage, separation; adolescence
    and troubled maturity:

having served under that bright sky you may look up
    but don't ask too much:
some cold beer, a few old friends in the afternoon,
    a Southerly Buster at dusk.

Caroline Caddy
Cosmos

I have a daughter.
I have a son.
They are two galaxies
                that shrink and grow
                            and spit stars.
I red-shift them spin them off
                            my spiral arms—
smaller larger Magellanic clouds.
I have a daughter.

I have a son.
They are comets
                    that exist by turning
                                    their long plumes
away from me.
I revolve slower and slower
                    still in the heat
                                    that began them
and blows their beauty from me.
I have a daughter.
I have a son.
In my worn out space-ship I crash land
                    crawl out and make my way
(invisible blob trailing pixie dust)
to the town.
First take the shape of one
                                    and live in her eyes.
Then take the shape of the other
                                    feel through his heart
without changing a hair
                                    how can I
                                            let them know
I am only taking as much as I need
                                    to effect repairs—
                                            won't stay
but space-borne again
                    will always be
                                    apogeed perigeed
                                            to them.

Joanne Burns
Australia

she was going snorkelling for scallops. she went most sundays in
the summer. soft fleshy scallops made a great meal on warm
dreamy sunday nights. the local papers said the day would be
fine and mild. a nice day for the children to play on the beach,

building sandcastles while she and her husband were in the water. they had four young daughters. they were hoping for a son in eight months time. five children would be enough to manage they had decided. it made the future easier to plan for.

the national papers the next morning reported that she had been taken by a huge shark. there had been a splash. she had been bitten in half. a retired fisherman watching from a cliff said he saw a big spray and red froth and bubbles. he said the shark was longer than a rescue boat. there were no remains of her; just one of the flippers. this absence of human remains was unprecedented.

the newspapers said her four young daughters had stood far away on the shore watching. they had been building a moat for their sandcastle. the report said the girls were one hundred and fifty metres away; that the father was two hundred metres away; the papers said the shark was six metres long. the newspapers were full of figures. as if someone was desperate to fill in the gaps.

for the next few nights right across the nation people's dreams were full of strange and terrible holes; while the pacific ocean remained blue in every atlas in the world

Diane Fahey
Andromache

Heroes widow their wives, who must embrace paradox:

After he left, I was with him all the time;
his every ache, deprivation, I felt before he did.

When the messenger came, I told *him* the news;
only the details of death needed to be named.

Now they drift through our home like flakes of ash,
or buzz like stunned flies around my head.

Sunlight invades each room, shadows the hearth;
somewhere, a storm splinters the air.

The house is utterly empty, it is thronging with presences;
weeping, I cannot hear my voice, which is everywhere.

After a hero closes his eyes, people keep him awake forever;
when I close my eyes, I see the years I have lived—

a felled avenue of trees; I see the years ahead—
dark birds watching me, circling me, giving me

more and more time.

Thirteen

I was practising being a saint.
My brown lace-ups were clamped
to the dusty floor, and I was in them.
The mirror, an oval drop
of flat untrembling water, showed
a pale girl inside a yellow raincoat.
I hated it. 'This one,' I said.
My mother passed the silky beige one,
the dearer one, back to the woman,
and softly they agreed: 'Too young
to know its value.'
                                    'Some of us even
wear yellow raincoats to school!'
The nun stood on a bench—
wasp-waisted, her cheeks covered
with tributaries of red lightning.
Her eyes glittered as two hundred girls
marched with military precision
round the playground. In tune
with a deeper instinct, I dragged
my feet into the asphalt,
waiting to be detected, punished…
She was the one who ground me down
the way she ground her yellow teeth,
and almost triumphed—
until the day when, kindled with rage,

she struck me across the arm:
'Get out, then!' And I had won,
my eyes drops of flat untrembling water,
giving her back her hatred,
polishing it with the fresh shine of youth.

Robert Gray
Diptych

1

My mother told me how one night, as would often happen,
    she'd stayed awake
in our board house, at the end of a dark, leaf-mulched drive,
waiting for my father, after the pubs had closed,
knowing he would have to walk
miles, 'in his state',
if no one would bring him home
(since, long before this, he had driven his own car off a
    mountain-side,
and, becoming legend, had rode
on the knocked-down banana palms
of a plantation, right to the foot, and someone's door,
the car reared high on a great raft of mutilated, sap-oozing fibre;
from which he'd climbed down, unharmed, his most soberly
    polite,
and never driven again).
This other night, my mother was reluctant to go out, and leave
    us kids asleep,
and fell asleep herself, clothed, on the unopened bed,
but leapt upright, sometime later, the most foul taste
in her mouth—glimpsed at once
he was still not there—and rushed out, gagging,
to find that, asleep, she'd bitten off the tail
of a small lizard, dragged through her lips. That bitterness
    (I used to imagine),
running onto the verandah to spit,

and standing there, spat dry, seeing across the silent, frosty bush
the distant lights of town had died.

And yet my mother never ceased from what Heidegger
    invokes—from extending Care
(although she'd only ever read the *Women's Weekly*,
and though she could be 'damned grumpy' through a few
    meal-times, of course).
This care for things, I see, was her one real companion
in those years.
It was as though there were two of her,
an harassed person, and a calm, that saw what needed to be
    done, and
seemed to step through her, again.
Her care you could watch reappear like the edge of tidal water
in salt flats, about everything.
It was this made her drive out the neighbour's bull from our
    garden with a broom,
when she saw it trample her seedlings—
back, step by step, she forced it, through the broken fence,
it bellowing and hooking either side sharply at her all the way,
    and I
five years old on the back steps calling
'Let it have a few old bloody flowers, Mum.'
No. She locked the broom handle straight-armed across its nose
and was pushed right back herself, quickly, across the yard. She
ducked behind some tomato stakes,
and beat it with the handle, all over that deep hollowness of the
    muzzle,
poked with the millet at its eyes,
and had her way, drove it out bellowing; while I,
in torment, stood slapping into the steps, the rail, with an
    ironing cord,
or suddenly rushed down there, and was quelled, also,
repelled to the bottom step, barracking. And all,
I saw, for those little flimsy leaves
she fell to at once, small as mouse prints, amongst the chopped-
    up loam.

Whereas, my father only seemed to care that he would never
    appear a drunkard
while ever his shoes were clean.
A drunkard he would define as someone who had forgotten the
    mannerisms
of a gentleman. The gentleman, after all, is only known,
only exists, through manner. He himself had the most perfect
    manners,
of a kind. I can imagine no one
with a manner more easily, and coolly, precise. With him,
this manner had subsumed all of feeling. To brush and dent the
    hat
which one would doff, or to look about, over each of us, and
    then unfold a napkin
to allow the meal, in that town where probably all of the men
would sit to eat of a hot evening without a shirt,
was his passion. After all, he was a university man
(though ungraduated), something more rare then. My father, I
    see, was hopelessly melancholic—
he lived in some place far beyond an Edward Thomas. The
    position of those wary
small eyes, and thin lips,
on the long-boned face
proclaimed the bitterness of every pleasure, except those of
    form.
He mostly drank alone
at the RSL club, and had been known to wear a carefully-
    considered tie
to get drunk in the sandhills, watching the sea.
When he was ill and was at home at night, I would look into
    his bedroom,
at one end of a gauzed verandah,
from around the door and a little behind him,
and would see his frighteningly high-domed skull under the
    lamp-light, as he read

in a curdle of cigarette smoke.
Light shone through wire mesh onto the packed
    hydrangea-heads,
and on the great ragged mass of insects, like bees over a comb,
    that crawled tethered
and ignored right beside him. He seemed content, at these
    times,
as though he'd done all that he could to himself,
and had been forced, objectively, to give up.
He liked his bland ulcer-patient food
and the big heap of library books I had brought.
    (My instructions always were:
'Nothing whingeing. Nothing by New York Jews;
nothing by women, especially the French; nothing
translated from the Russian.')
And yet, the only time I actually heard him say that he'd
    enjoyed anything
was when he spoke of the bush, once. 'Up in those hills,'
he advised me, pointing around, 'when the sun is coming out of
    the sea, standing amongst
that tall timber, you can feel at peace.'
I was impressed. He asked me, another time, that when he died
I should take his ashes somewhere, and not put him with the
    locals into the cemetery.
I went up to one of the hills he had named
years earlier, at the time of day he had spoken of, when the
    half-risen sun
was as strongly-spiked as that one
on his Returned Soldier's badge,
and I scattered him there, utterly reduced at last, amongst the
    wet, breeze-woven grass.
For all his callousness to my mother, I had long accepted him.
After all, he'd given, or shown me, the best advice,
and had left me alone. And I'd come by then to think that
    everyone is pathetic.
Opening his plastic, brick-sized box, that morning,
my pocket-knife slid

sideways and pierced my hand—and so I dug with that one
into his ashes, which I found were like a mauvish-grey marble
    dust,
and felt that I needn't think of anything else to say.

Gillian Hanscombe
A Great Australian Family circa 1960

He Big Boss Breadwinner, first in lavatory (reads *The Sun*), first
in shower, first at breakfast, first with demands-commands, first
with announcements-pronouncements, first to phone, first to
front door, first out.

> *Father, mother, sister, sister;*
> *Flatter, mutter, whisper, whisper;*

Sister-secret is the youngest. She big little croucher, in and out
of shower, in and out of school-bag, in and out of wardrobe, in
and out of infinite tapestries of discretions. *If you don't tell you
don't know*, I taunt. *Won't know then*, she hints. She looks side-
ways out of her eyes. She creeps last out.

> *Father, mother, sister, sister;*
> *Flatter, mutter, whisper, whisper;*

I big deal bombardier. Watch out. I can crash-crush, revel-rage,
take aim, fire at will. I can get expelled. I can be longest in
shower, last at breakfast, least able to keep mysteries to myself.
I leave when I like.

> *Father, mother, sister, sister;*
> *Flatter, mutter, whisper, whisper;*

She Big Time Housewife, still in dressing-gown, cooking up a
storm, full of pain-complain, worry-flurry, duty-booty. When
they've all gone she cleans up, reads *The Sun*, eats buttered
toastcrusts, drinks tea. It's eight hours before cooking starts
again. What to wash? What to shop? What to plan? Who to
phone?

> *Father, mother, sister, sister;*
> *Flatter, mutter, whisper, whisper;*

At the time, it was narcotic, miasmic, surreptitiously mimetic.
The barometer measured working, smirking, striving, thriving,
obsession-confession, confusion-delusion, though the sun boiled
on and we all spoke underwater.

> *Father, mother, sister, sister;*
> *Flatter, mutter, whisper, whisper;*

In current daylight, with common hindsight, it's easy: the air is
thin, clear, companionably cold, comparatively calm; and all
that tense, dense, blood-bonded, four-square double-duet is
safely past, safely housed, safely honed, heeded, hoarded,
boarded;

> safely memorised.

> *Father, mother, sister, sister;*
> *Flatter, mutter, whisper, whisper.*

Mark O'Connor

The Dance Floor in the Cave—Kanangra Walls

Folk came riding from two days round,
breakfast at the cousins', then 'Off to the dance!'
Trotting up by the Thurat spires,
a last boulder-turn on the stock-path and
Hooley Dooley!—a cave
with a smooth plank floor, a fiddler and lanterns.
'Partners please…' for the genealogy waltz.

The rocks full of shell, like an ancient sea
moved lights in the ladies' eyes;
and the rhythmic moon of the violin,
glancing yellow in the overhang
made the finest sounds ever. And there was water,
sinking through sixty foot of sandstone
to plop in a barrel.
They danced till a pale light came up
through the tree-tops below. And after,
on coffee or whisky they rode home sleepless, to milking.
No one stole that plank-floor.

Dancing was serious business
—it could leave you courting
four days' ride away. And those eddying seas
would be life-time tides,
discussed and fathered and aunted over
before any step beyond this floor—and though its wood
is charcoal in some camper's fire,
many a stout old trunk survives in nursing homes
known to a score of grandchildren.

Peter Skrzynecki
Feliks Skrzynecki

My gentle father
Kept pace only with the Joneses
Of his own mind's making—
Loved his garden like an only child,
Spent years walking its perimeter
From sunrise to sleep.
Alert, brisk and silent,
He swept its paths
Ten times around the world.

Hands darkened
From cement, fingers with cracks
Like the sods he broke,
I often wondered how he existed
On five or six hours' sleep each night—
Why his arms didn't fall off
From the soil he turned
And tobacco he rolled.

His Polish friends
Always shook hands too violently,
I thought . . . *Feliks Skrzynecki,*
That formal address
I never got used to.
Talking, they reminisced

About farms where paddocks flowered
With corn and wheat,
Horses they bred, pigs
They were skilled in slaughtering.
Five years of forced labour in Germany
Did not dull the softness of his blue eyes.

I never once heard
Him complain of work, the weather
Or pain. When twice
They dug cancer out of his foot,
His comment was: 'but I'm alive'.

Growing older, I
Remember words he taught me,
Remnants of a language
I inherited unknowingly—
The curse that damned
A crew-cut, grey-haired
Department clerk
Who asked me in dancing-bear grunts:
'Did your father ever attempt to learn English?'

On the back steps of his house,
Bordered by golden cypress,
Lawns—geraniums younger
Than both parents,
My father sits out the evening
With his dog, smoking,
Watching stars and street lights come on,
Happy as I have never been.

At thirteen,
Stumbling over tenses in Caesar's *Gallic War*,
I forgot my first Polish word.
He repeated it so I never forgot.
After that, like a dumb prophet,
Watched me pegging my tents
Further and further south of Hadrian's Wall.

Kornelia Woloszczuk

Her face
Betrays the darkness of storms,
Winds that alter
The outline of a coast—
Eyes to outstare
The face of the waters:
As if hands
Were dragging
The depths of a swamp
In search
Of her lost son.

Being
Her only child,
Where did I go wrong?
Not knowing
The cave of silence
In which
She outwaited
Tides of absence, seas
Of loneliness
That lapped her dress
Like a prayerwheel,
Confined to the centre
Of a wasteland
On her palms?

In springtime
She walks beside
A river, pointing out
How water destroys images
That reflect eternity:
Grassblades, leaves, flowers—
At whose roots
A fire burns
When a man forsakes
His wife and child.

Her feet
Make no imprint
Upon the grass
She treads.

Walking
Behind her
I listen for birdcalls,
Look at breaking water
With every fish in air—
Nervous, uncertain
Of distances and colours
We pass through.
A dream, she says,
Is the path from God:
A faith to cherish
What you inherit
At birth—sustain the winds
On which prophets spoke
Across seas
And ruins of hills.
All is sacrificed
For the sake of children
Who forget you
Before you are dead—

But, remember,
'Having only one child
Is like having
One eye in your head.'

Bobbi Sykes
Miscegenation

Excuse me / sir—

Are you my father?
I've searched so hard to find you.
I need to know / you understand /
Life's been so hard without you.

Excuse me / sir—

> Please...
> Are *you* my daddy?
> You could be—she said brown hair /
> And that I'd know you anywhere.

Excuse me / sir—

> Are *you* my father?
> Mother always cried /
> Rather than speak of you /
> So I know nothing /
> Except that I am here...

Excuse me / sir—

> Are you my daddy?
> I hope you won't mind if I ask /
> Was it love—or was it loathing?
> I know nothing / you understand?
>
> Did you love her? Really love her?
> Stroke her hair, hold her hand?
>
> Or was she just another roll /
> Or rape? Did she cry?
> I'll understand!

Excuse me /sir—

> Did you become her lover /
> Accidentally /
> As drunks often do?
> Is that how I came to be?
> O / please / please—tell me...

Excuse me / sir—

> I always wanted my daddy /
> You know how it is with girls /
> But I grew up without lace and ribbons /
> Just my mind—all in a whirl.

Excuse me / sir—

> I badly need to find /
> Not for any real reason /
> I'm not asking for money / you know /
> It would just make a world of difference /
> To have a father that I could know.

Excuse me / sir—

> Are *you* my daddy?
> I've been searching everywhere /
> It doesn't matter if you don't love me /
> And I won't tell anyone, I swear.

Excuse me / sir—

> I've looked through the north / the west /
> Doing the country—town by town /
> My Mum was Black / my Dad was White /
> And that's why I'm this brown.

Excuse me / sir—

> If you are not my father /
> Have you seen him anywhere?
> I'd love to find my daddy /
> Just to meet him / just to see him /
> Just to know that he's somewhere…

Excuse me / sir

> Excuse me / sir

>> Excuse me / sir.

Shelton Lea

And So They've Murdered Julia's Lawn

and so they've murdered julia's lawn.
sitting there on a sunday morning with vanessa
breaking our night-long fast
in the sun as bright as a fresh cadaver,

when this idiot in ear muffs comes in
and begins to murder the lawn.

my breakfast failed to amuse me
as my mouth was all agape.
this guy, just off the street, comes into the garden
with his mower
and starts to murder the lawn.
and it was spring, when all the weeds begin to flower
with their pale pistils, portentous, pointing at the dawn
and this silly bugger in his yellow ear muffs
has come and proceeded to murder julia's lawn.

so i gets off my seat and starts to yell
but he can't hear me because of his muffs
and I run across what's left of julia's lawn,
pluck from his ears the offensive silence
and tell him to go get stuffed. leave the lawn alone.

and mind you this is only just after dawn.

Eric Beach

Hollowcourt Centre for Intellectually Disabled Adults

Melanie's allowed to be on her own
she's sewn pieces of mirror together like an afghan jacket
cut out magazine girls in melodramatic poses
they crinkle on a pasted sea
she points—'she's happy, she can go anywhere she likes'
her mother bashed her into idiocy
now she draws red lines on her own pale skin
'I promise God' she says 'that one day I'll forgive myself'

George slumps on his bed, complain, complain
'I'm always thirsty, doctor told them I need my vitamins'
nurses avoid him, wheelchairs parked a floor below
'I want to go home' whines George 'mum needs me'
I need not tell him that she's dead

his room-mate does, clever enough to be nasty
'thirsty George?' he cackles 'you had a bath didn't you?'

Peter smiles like a sun in an airless room
it's taken me six weeks to reach his name
when I leave, I know he'll retreat into a silence
no name can call back
I repeat stories as though they're rituals
dinner here lasts ten minutes
a man flings two lumps of bread on each plate

Mary stands too close to people, talking at them
'my mind' she says 'my mind & me'
she says 'if only we could make friends'
she wants to be married & have children
but children here are sudden weight losses
our local newspaper had her smiling, one hand stretched out of
    frame
rustling her plastic bag full of plastic bags

Once was Always

once was always where my young river roared
out of high-windowed nights down steep new days
tugged to a knot, white knuckled
down a dream ladder, out over a wall poured smoother
than a skin of secrets
where dull water bumps now in tree-tops
I moved against my love's soft light

my small drowned town where doors once opened swung
outwards forever, my packed entrances
now in a suitcase in th hall
th crown & anchor board behind th china cabinet
where I won ha'pennies
(granddad's gas shillings in a brown jar)
my aunt's milk squirt in my wide eye

jealous gods lie, th awkward ache of arms
round loose-necked babies was no drowning bath

each new child a shock of love
my brother's trusting hand, sister crying for a tune
I played my chanter
bagpipes & nanny's chooks laid more eggs
I peeled th apple of my eye

while gabby women in storied houses
flicked sharp tongues to eat a buzz of gossip
'little pitchers have big ears'
men sank from sight in their weighty world, they came at dark
pipes hooked in their lips
survivors of currents, motionless
pockets of silver, spilling worlds

A Scrapbook of Sun

I oiled & powdered you sparrow fart pink
cradled your bob head so carefully
you were a buoy & I an aching sea

& love's sure tide came flooding in
when you ran to me, tottering
on a grin, determined

& like an old blues, love changed
'you can't stop it running out'
your mother answered your doubts strangely

'your dad had to leave to write poetry'
this sort of over-simplicity
might better explain my absence

& my long silence, your hair turned blonde
to black, your mother's dark eyes
a smile I recognised

in photos, a news clipping
of you saving a drowning dog at ten
& giving his owner a piece of your mind

in your last year you worked for life-line
a children's cancer ward, tried
for paid jobs, died

one night from pills, kind verdict
accidental, your funeral
a mixture of laughter & tears

three people attended who said
they'd found you a job
you were ahead

Kristin Henry
On Learning That Mothers Die

She is cooking frenchfries.
Cutting huge potatoes into slices,
slices into fingers,
six long and straight-edged,
two short crescent thumbs.
'Everybody has to in the end' she says,
careful not to splatter.
Still the crazy oil hisses.
In the days before career
she wore naive aprons,
wide-sashed and butterfly-bowed.
I watch her back.

'But not you.' (Who's worried?
Absurd, a world without her.)
I love this new green dress especially.
Before she sewed she drew a picture
of it, on me. See,
just like Cinderella.
I'm not worried.
'Well, one day, sure.'
She keeps dropping in the raw white sticks.

Each time there's applause inside the pot.
Another Idaho is stripped
and sacrificed before she turns around.

I have covered my face with my skirt
and will never take it away.
No one can make me.
'Oh, not for a long, long time' she soothes.
What's that supposed to mean
on the scale of a five year old?
Dad comes home to me
under my green veil,
my immature mourning.
Mother is about to cry or protest,
knowing she's guilty of murder.
And the room is filling with black smoke.

Peter Kocan
The Little Garrisons

Here is a dull suburban avenue,
A row of houses of the middling sort.
This is where the vast collapse has come to,
And this is where the war is being fought.

Here are the people doing what they can
As friend and neighbour, parent, husband, wife,
Continuing against the odds to man
The little garrisons of normal life.

Along the street's perimeter they link
The small acts of meaning and of beauty.
In rooms, in gardens, at the kitchen sink,
They stand to their customary duty.

History will bring their story home,
Will liken them to those heroic ranks
Who held the last of Athens and of Rome
And fought without encouragement or thanks.

But now the quiet valour of the day
Is just to win another night ahead,
To get the dishes washed and put away,
And tuck the anxious children into bed.

Rhyll McMaster
Washing the Money

At weekends, my father and younger sister
scrubbed the Queen's obdurate lips in the bathroom basin
where plain soap, warm water
made money a clean creation.
The silk grease of pounds, maroon tint of 'fivers',
the crisper starch of a ten shilling note
snapped and capered under his fingertips.

I saw millions of unmatched fingerprints,
bone transparent, brittle snail shells
bump around the rim.
Nothing strange in washing the currency
which lay exhausted like strained, wet cabbage.

Then they ironed it dry between best linen tea towels
while my mother hovered, grim;
'Oh darl,' she said, 'don't singe them.'
Puffs of rich steam jumped up
over that pair of alchemists' shoulders
who, oblivious, never asked
if she meant the tea towels or the money.

Holiday House

The Austin A-40 called 'Michael' always made it
with the five of us, ports, mosquito nets,
the car floor heating till it burnt our feet
and the dachshund in grave peristalsis slung on our knees.

Mum always jammed her own cutlery under the seat springs—
when the dog tried to wriggle to heaven we had visions
of sliced Windsor never blood.

Once over Narrowneck
everything seemed white and golden. The car nosed left
at the hotel with porthole windows
its brick cupola like a diver's helmet
out of the *Children's Encyclopedia*.

Parked over our grease-spot from last year
we raced to be first to catch sand beetles,
'keeping the place neat'.
At night in our beds, on damp sheets,
hair sticky with salt, sand on our feet, mozzie nets
down against Scotch Greys,
we heard the sea at high tide.
It boomed, it slurred up the beach. It whispered in space.
It sniffed at the dunes and climbed our dream windows.

My Mother and I Become Victims of a Stroke

Lost

'For once in my life,'
she says, 'on my empty feet.'
'For once in my life
give me something'
and looks at me with yearning,
bland old eyes.
'I've never had
not once, not once!' she shouts
but the sentence scoots away
before she can struggle with it.

'I just need a vimsin tripe,'
she says, putting teabags in the toilet
quite surprised
to find cheese sweating in the biscuit tin
the Nescafe jar full of water.

'You need a rest
you're my daughter,'
she smiles and tells an inside joke
that ends instead in tears.
She shuts all doors and windows.
She'd lose the keys if she was given them.
Her hard-held territory
full of unidentified badmen
who jeer, nod and disappear.

She stares in the mirror
adjusts her glasses
a drawer full of oddments at her feet.
She needs a decade
to sort through all she has collected.
'I can't with my fat head,' she cries.
'Disgusting.

'It's no good.
It's folded up—a damn shame.
Look at me!
I used to be a young girl.'
Her voice fades. She leans one elbow
on her bed, quite conversational.
She peers at me over a pinnacle of handbags.
'I've lost everything now,' she says.

David Reiter
Cats Slip In

1

Cats slip into the gap: between shrub
and fence, lid and can, leg and screen,
absent parent and child. They patrol
the suburbs for indecision, dangling
mouse-pelts before our averted eyes
like leaflets urging verandah baptism.

Before the split, I conceded no gaps
for cats. The neighbours suspected
subversion—*three children and no
 pets?* But the flag of my daughter's
asthma silenced them to sympathy
like men who think in mistresses.

On access days now, I trip over cats
at the gate. My daughter, I'm told,
is miraculously healed of all that I
denied her: she absorbs adrenalin
from her mother's heat. The fur
she strokes sighs like a sleepy father.

Graham Rowlands
From *Jeremy's Poems*
The Curls

They're coming off, I'm afraid.
The blond ringlets springing
long enough for a pony tail's ribbon
are sprung, unsprung—can't
outlast his second candle.

His relatives trim their remarks.
Just a bit. Only an inch or so.
The woman feeding peanuts to the monkeys
offers the girl a biscuit. He accepts.
The boys & girls at child care
think he's a girl. Even the doctor
has to confirm a boy's a boy
before lighting up his ears.
I can take it, of course. I'm a big boy.

I wouldn't side with the short back & sides
if only I could forget that photo of
Oscar Wilde in a dress at how old?
& how, towards the end
the wallpaper was killing him.

The Hypocrite

Yes, son, I know you
learned them all from me
& your mother. I'm
buggered if I was going
to stop swearing
just because I was
feeding you yoghurt
in your highchair.
That's when I swore most.
No, of course I'm not saying
I didn't swear before
you were born. You don't
think I learned them all from *you*
do you. Bloody ridiculous.
I wasn't born yesterday
even if you *were*. Christ!
I know you weren't born yesterday.
I was there. I'm sorry.
Let's get to the point.
You can say anything you like
here. This is your *home*.
You can probably get away with it
in the playground too—depending
on which teacher is on duty.
But everywhere else, son
(are you listening?)
everywhere else
I want you to be
a fucking hypocrite. Okay?
(H Y P O C R I T E)

Lily Brett
Children (I)

You
mother
would have

like
all
the other
mothers

gone
with
the
children

held
their
hands

hushed
their
cries

smoothed
their
hair

pulled
a pullover
into place

jammed
in

they
held
their children

to
breathe
the last air

the
gas
burst
from the ceiling

hitting
them
first.

I Wear Your Face

You never recovered
and I
and others mother
wear your burden

hugging it to me
like a collapsed cloak
a tattered coat

I wear your wariness
can't hug another
mother

I wear the glare
you froze me
with

I wear your desperation
and carry
warring strangers within myself

I wear your fear
with practised ease
pleasing you

I wear your face
and mother
the green witch howls behind it.

Jeff Guess
Present Imperfect

on the morning notices   heavily accented in blue
    teachers please note   'Jennifer Cain's father
is very seriously ill   please keep this in mind'

as she has for the last months   her face creased
    wrongly for crying   she holds it set
strangely now   struggling to follow
    why she is always mixing up her tenses
until now   nodding as the marks on the page get too red
    for something she cannot put right   alone
like wiping the mess with the dark blood   from his
    pyjamas this morning   and holding his weak tea
while her mother rang the doctor   Jennifer Cain
    made no mistakes in her life   but it would not let her pass
before his pain   laid waste in her   an innocence

Kate Jennings
Assassin

A baby squalling. A rodent squealing.
The phone. We capsize into consciousness.

A woman, neither young nor old,
Southern accent, panicked, pleading.

She wants to speak to my husband,
'Yes?' he asks, into the receiver.

As always on waking, his face has
the creased innocence of a newborn.

'Nobody there.' I try. 'Hello. Hello.'
No intake of breath, no echo.

A still silence. A back road
on a cloudless winter's night.

Click. Dial tone. I wait, fully
expecting my emotions to bolt,

but feel only sisterhood
with a woman whom need

has made a bottom dweller:
headlight eyes, bag-needle teeth.

Her belly! It distends to three times
her size to accommodate her prey.

The next morning, my husband says
he has no idea who the caller was.

We speculate as to her identity,
and then, because it is laundry day,

strip the bed. A minor argument
erupts: he likes patterned sheets,

I have a preference for plain.
We fold and tuck. Fluff and plump.

Tony Lintermans
The Shed Manifesto

No matter how grand his house—shed with icing—
or winning his wife—enemy of sheds, usually—
whatever his car, career, position, a man's shed
is coagulation, unburdened essence of himself.
It is also the shed itself.

Hard men can weep in sheds, honking and snuffling
for half an hour or more before composing
a face to meet the world. The shed understands.
Hasn't it always been adjunct, backyard dweller,
cat-smeared, overcoat-infested outcast?

The shed is home to the humble. What dero
drifting under alcoholic stars, wanting
a little warmth, has not dreamed
of stumbling through that dark aperture (for the best
sheds have no doors) to sleep on wheat bags, tarps,
snug in the smell of old dust and kerosene drums?
The first religion—love of children—engendered sheds.
The second—idolatry of speed—ends there
in brittle riding tack and horseshoes hanging from nails,
gaskets, dead batteries, engines dismembered and scattered
and sometimes, in back country where the faith has good duco
entire cars on blocks, an offering to Shed.

Shed has known love, but doesn't like to talk about it.
But will, if its rusted reticence is pressed, unloose
(for sheds experienced in love have doors, and further doors)
antique aromas, delicate bat flutterings, unidentifiable dews,
a stew of memories cooling in the dark, tyre-balding interior.
Sometimes it is better not to ask.

The shed, like the nose, is too obvious for History
but no conquest starts without it. Is it accident
that settlement begins with sheds, breezy First Fleeters
of terra firma, while timid cities follow?
That Christ first breathed in a shed? That Alexander
burst, unbeatable, from good shed-breeding country?
Tyrants are those who have forgotten sheds, or prefer,
like Genghis, to sleep in a tent. May they rot in earth
unblessed by sheds, forever rocking their marble regrets.
The shed does not forget.

When men forget, the shed is subtle reminder.
A man needing a one-eighth drill bit can search the shed
for hours, looking first in likely places—pockets
of mouldy reefer jackets, small cities
of silverfish in empty alum boxes, a child's shoe
(its owner long a lawyer) waiting to be glued—then
in possible spots—above the beam where washers rot,

for instance, the hollow insides of handlebars, until
despair reducing him to hopeless gestures,
he looks in the drawer marked 'Drill etcetera'.

It's there (for a wife, generally, has no feeling
for the proper placement of tools). Enraged, crazed
a junk diaspora ensues. Boxes of bolts go flying,
blunt scythes attempt shed shortening, a tail shaft
becomes battering ram, the cat a witness, cowering.
Exhaustion settles with the dust.
The search for the one-eighth drill bit
begins again. A man will look in the shed
and find himself.

Shed is freedom, the soul's aquarium where
memory eddies and the day stands still.
Oh ship of cobwebs riding the busy hills,
your intimate cargo sleeping steady, bedded
in sump oil seeping through dust, how can I
praise you enough? How lucky the snake
that slides inside whenever it likes, to feel your flesh
(for the shed has shadows, and the shadows have weight)
brushing against its skin!

The world with its warnings—Stay away from Shed!
The shed eats everything!—grows wearisome.
What can a complex organ feed on, if not
unquenchable life in objects? I tack this list
of virtues to its walls, hammering gently
so the wood won't crack, and step back happy.

Shed approves.
Sheets of roof iron move between their nails.
A paint tin pops. Rafters take up their tiny slack.
Shed is murmuring!

The snake, awake and sensing politics, stops
to interpret, to squiggle in the dust:
Vote One, SHED.

John A. Scott
The Passing, at Boho
FOR ALAN GOULD

By night a pester-wind.
Awakening from oversleep, uncommonly, to find
the generator's *nag-nag-nag* grown still
with sun, the knowledge took her wandering,
shocked among the hollow cars, her body
scribbled with a slow red ant thoroughness
of rust: her father's heart was wearing out.

By evening as a child—at Boho,
all the creek trees under veils of white moth,
married—bellied on the dark
damp grass, she'd watch the moons:
the front door porthole window full
against a drifting weatherboard;
and that other, rising with its roll
of cow's eye, slice of whiteness, terrified
before the hammers. Before the city spat
the road gangs there.
                Her genitals
concerned her only twice. A tar-man,
acrid blue, had clambered from her,
coughing, reaching for tobacco;
calling her undictionaried words.
The shade was pitiless; the metal
dashboard fuming; breathing alcohol.
Only twice. And both with pain.
A single child that tore her 'being made'
and tore her once again at birth. And now
she'd done with them.
                   'Up there!' she
screamed. 'You see her coming, 'pie?'
Its wing-stroke metred, wind stressed
through the morning shimmer. And out

along those web-paths, do you see the widow
come to take the males that worship her?
All night the pester-wind. She'd hear
the whispering approach. Another darkness
shuffling home, to eat.

Her daughter drove
the Boho road. *Unresting me. Calling me*
from sleep as once she might've years ago.
The landscapes of her childhood, heard
in sombre clock silences. The static
of a radio, breaking; held against
the ear: a sea. My only child (and like
my mother, fatherless) my daughter;
smoked away to nothing; with her child-
face rising through the window, far
across the paddocks caught in rain-hush.
Out of season.
But now the road was closed.
The metal spikes hammer-pierced
through bitumen: a regimented black and
white of barricade, too hot to touch.
She heard the distant freeway, derisive
with its smear of passing traffic.
I am so bright with likenesses, she
thought, that I could cry.

She walked
a time upon the porch, the weight held back
against her spine; a dress puckered with
its handful clutchings. *Don't tug so, child!*
Don't tug so!
The clouds were muscular,
relentless in their manhood, that by
evening bore tattoos of bird-flight.
'Up there!' she cried. 'You see her, 'pie!'
Her body pierced. Spread against the
chisel of the grasses or a first edge

of uncommon rain. Either way that bore
—indelibly—the face of men. *I beat
my fists against him and they stuck.*

These roads, she thought. What tar-based
poison am I carrying. Staring out across
the gathering change. *There are so many
names for evening, child, for half-light
I've awoken.*

             And so she sat, alone upon
the porch, within the rocking-chair's
cane ampersand, quietly joining generations:
   light to shadow, day to night.

Alex Skovron
Beyond Nietzsche

'...an infant's littlest, purest love: the kind
born of the moment, not the mind.'

I

Tonic/dominant, tonic/dominant...
One ambulance crushes a thousand ants,
dozing pedestrians pass, or gaping
blunder against each other. A distinguished
father prides himself on self-control, is
irritated, drags his daughter
into a doorway. Tantrum unleashed
he desperately tugs, she lashes out, strikes:
he stuns her with a blow that breaks
his heart for weeks.

Across the road a poet, drunk
in the act of a risky procreation,
pauses. A siren is headed
for a fire, he lifts a shutter
like a half-meant apology, recalls a poem
he never wrote, returns

to his mug of scotch, the corpse
hot to his hand, his aetiology. *The Age
of Reason* hovers half-open by the bed,
her breath is thick.

A list of ants attack
a jamstain on the sink. I drum
the hollow stainless steel to startle them,
they scatter. Finger lightly licked
I pluck the stragglers, flick them in the grass
out the back door. Later
(three a.m.) my baby son squirms
like an insect at my neck.
How easily your children can expose you,
if you listen.

II

Like the stick sun of a small child
every word announces a spindle
of meanings.

An oboe's rim is riddled with minutest creatures;
the calligrapher's sac dispenses
a death-black fluid. Home with child
the heart of Übermensch is bursting
with goodwill: he listens to Requiem K.626
on his gramophone, ponders the meaning
of its dark beauty.
                    Tonic/dominant...

Like the rippling pebble of a gazing child
each note unlocks a sun system
of meanings...

III

But the ripples will quickly subside,
only the stone will know the weight of the water.
A spiderweb is infinitely trivial:

sitting and patiently waiting,
only the spider…

So every meaning conspires against itself
till the littlest love alone can defy meaning,
and every word that makes the world
is half a moon hiding among absent stars.
Each truth is a half-moon;
the minutest love alone can escape meaning.

IV

And the galaxies—how swiftly they flick past
on the black train
torpedoing unalterably across the night
in the next suburb…It is possible
the shriek that disintegrates a dream means
merely whistle, and a train,
isn't it?

I know a world
where every truth shelters a thousand lies,
each noble thought holds off a swarm of savages
again, and every smile disturbs
a labyrinth of doubts…Familiar world.
Sometimes, alone at night
listening for trains, I hear its ghostly dialectic.
Tonic/dominant, tonic/dominant…

And I long for a word free of all its meanings.
The littlest love.

Alan Wearne
From *Out There* (6)

Lorraine McNab, Marian's youngest sister, a radical nurse

Darling, the great McNab reception
has stopped. There was no marriage,
only a wedding which lapsed

into three children; and Marian's
one good thing arrives is over.

'Blowin' my millions!' puffed out
the boom-time father of
I and the bride. 'There's three to go!'
Now he unbends each weekend,
pale and gutty, with neat
imported whiskey. If I arrive he
calls me 'Commo Daughter',
asks after 'yer revolution',
he's part of it, wouldn't guess,
but listens to what etc, I'm saying,
smiles, disagrees and forgets it.

Out where I rarely attend,
(household clothed in Butterick designs,
as we were), my concerns would never, never
be welcome: my concepts, our concepts:
out there Marian and Russell Viney
are splitting, and nephew Brett has made
one mad grand design and gesture:
blood on the staff-room floor,
frankly delightful, but for the act.

I've no memories, just memory.
Can you still hear *Holiday for Strings,*
April in Portugal? If so,
I'm with mother, plotting our styles
and dress sense, copies of Australian Bride,
The English Bride, Bride America,
the radio's *Lunching and Listening* to
Moulin Rouge, Limelight, at a kid sisters'
fitting session. (School's nearly over,
Thursday and Friday disposed, off.)

I was the tomboy
junior bridesmaid, my love: the idea
of Bombe Alaska, my bane:

one of the younger Viney guests
chasing me, mad about kissin'.
But a kid controls a strange
differing past. Now this wedding
wasn't exactly Marian's Russell's
this, with its Bombe Alaska, kissin'.
No doubt Marian: fool sister fool spouse,
gazed as a cow into Russell
promising; her life's great happy day
at twenty, with trappings though,
to be Mrs Viney out there in
Horses Arse country, hoo-ray.

After their holiday: the visiting
—she took Jean and Marlene
into a room, Marl giggled me aside
—too young; all my thinking: of
an adventure, then this post-mortem
laid, unforgettable cheap,
her private life into a minor room
as a twelve-year-old, leant against the door,
sobbed, as it was vague sinister silly.
O why should I choose, ear-mark,
this for reference, re-reference?
Had I an analyst, the need for one,
he'd she'd total the event and yes!
Well she bought me a 'snow storm'.
it dropped and cracked in a week.

Am never terrified now and that's
'liberation', horrifying word, over-used
and abused. Some Saturday morning
tramp round the market and centres
bellowing 'our bodies' is a sign, sure,
though not one of utility, commitment.
And yes *I'm* doing something:
to work is to initiate to be (if you wish)
Radical; and slogans maybe brash cliquey.

'Present your views by all means,
present your views to the
market place of the world.' Thus father,
He treated the youngest the favourite
to matinees, would take me out
and watch some loud-mouth marine
take Iwo Jima like it was Real Estate
—action's what he wanted, gave;
I presume, an example:

The clinic is powerful, has
a half-way home to liaise with,
—my kin, imagine throwing sister
in with working wives (as she…)
well, thrown out by wallopings, not playboys,
who, in any event scream fuck-off
and leave. Perhaps out there,
it is the Viney rule, with those
poor men, deluded into payments, chicks…

For there has to be concern for Marian,
for my object-addicted, middle-ground,
mothering big sister. Let's not acting
but to act, for it's our age,
our life and times, and they're out,
smarmers with their wives and lurvers
…should always be…
hey, little girl, do you still
run to his arms and seek
as these songs? Marian you object,
they're telling you, telling
he's almost there: sister that's shit!

Mrs Russell Viney née McNab!
McNab! To have our parents' name
is to have a man's name,
strange really. We lack
continuity, unless like Marian

we latch and start off
at twenty with
further letters of the alphabet. But,
McNab, she'd be proud of that,
proud of father, out
hoarding prices for un-sewered,
un-paved un-forget it;
I keep the name, shall,
not as the irony, which I
alone appreciate, rather as
reminder. He's here, all
his representation, too,
more even than with big sister,
the prick playboy husband,
her distraught slashing and hacking
elder son. They are, she is a
Viney now, the wedding over.
I'm McNab, Lorraine McNab.

Kevin Brophy
Painting Session

She can't paint without taking her clothes off
and painting her body.
Beginning with her hands and finally covering
all she can reach,
pushing the paint in aboriginal circles,
she says,
'Look, now I have a blue belly.'

When I give her the containers to wash out
with a hose,
she licks them out,
seriously comparing the tastes of red, blue and yellow.

My bland contribution
is to remind her that if she mixes colours

all she'll have in the end is a muddy brown.
She nods like a wise monkey and disregards me.

I have a blue demon, blue-eyed, rolled in blue,
tonguing the blue air here in the yard.
I hose her back to something like my child.
I am calm, distant, middle-aged,
the colour barely showing in my face,
all colours flaring wildly between us.

Alan Gould
The Chairs of This House

Each secret of this family we know:
We are the shapes its forebears have abandoned.

We dream we graze on smoke or talk, or stand
like stony cattle watched by men in portraits.

Yet from us young men go to fetch their shotguns,
their cigarettes left smoking in the ashtrays,

and when no others will we take the lost
and close them dumbly in our serious arms.

It is the old who trust us most, who doze
deep in the distant place where here is then,

and dream how George's brave and modest speech
was integral with sunlight on a chairback,

how Clara's maddening shrug is incomplete
without this room's exactitude in mind.

And were we granted speech with you we'd say
that nothing placed in time is trivial.

But too far back to matter speech escaped us.
Now we stand like sad heraldic beasts

hoarding ear-rings, coins and matchsticks, hoarding
what is yours, our long experience.

Jamie Grant
Mon Père est Mort

For an oral exam, when aged thirteen,
my father was asked questions in French
by a visiting professor in trench-
coat and gold-rimmed spectacles, who was lean

with the thin, pursed lips of an enemy
interrogator. He pressed my father
to say what his father's *métier*
was—an awkward question, for how many

schoolboys know the French for 'Real Estate
Agent'? Adopting a tragic expression,
my father just replied *'Mon père est mort'*.

The professor blushed to commiserate;
when the results of the examination
were known, my father had the highest score.

Jennifer Maiden
In the Caesura

This air is good

                for closeness

& good too

                to taste on the limbs

as they run.

                The mountain sky

glitters grey

                with waterlight

through the lounge room.

                Air excites

as the water

                in air's coldness

speaks to water

                in the skin.

The baby wakes
in the lounge chair.
She was folded
feet crossed, as if
awaiting birth.
Now her wrist
turns & arches
as she studies it,
distracted by
its lazy elegance.
This the time
of day, the weather
now to sleep,
or to walk out
& meet the air,
the wet rims
of lived things, strong
& green & sleeping.
On my breast,
she curves her wrist,
lifts a lock
of my hair airily
& fans it
through her fingers.

Plastic Ponies
—after the anniversary of Tiananmen Square.

Even her own
love for them is wry, but
they shine in their basket, crisp
carnations
with curly pastel manes.
Some were made in China,
probably
by dissidents from prisons.
Some are threaded with glitter,

some have challenging tusks,
some raise arrogant nostrils,
some lower mild muzzles,
some have wings
                          and some dance
out their communion in her heart.
Sleek unicorns rear in air
and balance on strong tails.
Some glow indistinctly in the dark.
There are brown and grey dobbins
—more natural—which offer
the fingers a feel like clipped hair.
Together, we arrange them
in her dressing table mirror.
I have always mistrusted
dusty collectables: all dry
silk and vinyl blossom. These, however,
have stolen past my guard and stare
un-biodegradable
there, in their broken basket, poised
like free parts of a person, bare
carnations that can't self-express or die.

Vicki Raymond
Small Arm Practice
FOR MY PARENTS

Children can't understand
age's long-sightedness:
the book held at arm's length
seems a perverse joke.

Myopic peering at least
looks more reasonable:
you have to kneel
for a view of the rock pool.

How awkward it was in libraries
to sidle between a shelf
and some fool of a giant
browsing from two feet off!

Today I saw something
at a greater distance,
in the hard, summer colours
of a Christmas stamp:

two figures in a garden.
They were picking tomatoes.
The letter I was reading
plummeted out of focus.

Edith Speers

Open Letter to an Ex-defacto Postnuptial Cannibal

Kate had a husband;
she calls him Donald Duck,
but that's not you,
a sailor suit and a quack quack,
it's all too flat, too two-toned shoe
old-time cartoon cute—
that's not you.

Mary Ann had a husband;
she calls him shit face,
but that's not you,
a werewolf with tie-clip and drool,
it's all too gory, too tooth & nail
hunter and quarry a story—
that's not you.

I once had a husband of sorts;
I call him the Black Hole
because it's true,

an absence of light and an appetite,
it was all too much of nothing, too tight,
a dead end in outer space—
that's you.

Doris Brett
From Snow White's Stepmother

You must be watching very carefully, yourself
just as you watch others. Each morning
the body must be brought out and inspected,
dipped in the colourless god your magic
has perfected—reflected. Who is the fairest
one of all?

You grow up knowing that it's on your
hair and lips and nose that all
depends. You make a fly trap out of skin, spin
out of the king's sons' clammy kisses (those
murmurers of frogs turned into princes got it
wrong—it's quite reversed). You sweat,
you curse, you've heard of somewhere else
you think escape, it can't be worse. But there's
your governess, hare-lipped and humped,
intransigent camel, she's bred for the desert,
but you…? And see your aunts, the spinster
sisters who've licked themselves little as lizards—
the terrible grooming, the wounds…
Your father calls you 'Petal', your mother gives
you rouge to bloom and you stop thinking
of rooms where you may slowly
as roses enfold yourself, descend and enter,
(slow motion acrobat), the banned breathtaking
knowledge of your stem.

Well, you've hooked your king alright and then's
the struggle: The first wife—wafted like mothwing

over everything—dustdrift that never catches light;
her cursed offspring, and my husband, the king
besotted with her eyes. She spies.
I've seen her watching me and him.
'She's just a child,' he says, 'and artless'.
Artless as adders with her witching smile and pretty
manners. I've seen her catch her sight in mirrors
and, leaning in like lovers, tease it with turning
this way and that. She's burning with it
just beneath the skin. This ripening year will see
the blush beneath the cream.

And so you see I had to do it. Freed from her skin
mine renewed into satin—that old companion
of the years slank back—I could have been
twenty-three again, and almost happy, when
there's news from the forest: the non-slaughtered
daughter, and she living in miniature sin—seven
little men, and seven times seven if she'd found
them I'll be bound…Well, you know the rest,
the laces, comb and apple that she rose to take,
the fall, the death, and I
expecting that I'd solved it all…

But this time something was different.
I began to think about mirrors—the cold
skin—and what goes on under the undead
silver; and to image myself, Queen of the mirrors,
caverns behind the skin, hollow with waiting,
an ice-age dying to be spilled, to move
to bloom into water, fill, to be moonfuls
of moisture…
I spend the days waiting.
I dream of red moons, the stars bursting
out of line, expanding, my skin,
the silk of sex, the slippers burning,
and calling me to dance,
dance, dance myself to death.

John Forbes
The History of Nostalgia

The wish being father to the thought and mother
to your eager gestures—or at least the ones
a dulled sensibility remembers belonging to—you
stare off into the distance as hard as you can
as if some long desired form might materialise,
announcing just by its presence an end to change
& replacing this ridiculous static blur with
a perspective that creates a point of view—
something that slowly expands as you grow older,
broadening out like a real view does when you climb
a spur or wedge your way up a chimney: something
in short that doesn't tell you everything at once,
exhausting all its effects in a coup de théâtre
that explodes like a trick golf ball you address
to cane down the fairway. Instead it disappears
in a bright flash & a puff of smoke at your feet
so that you're left thinking, 'Can this be it?'
&, sure enough, it is—you're here, that's all,
another miserable subject, composed of a few jokes
& catchphrases worn smooth with repetition
but at the same time almost statuesque, like a bust
of yourself in marble or bronze & mounted on
that plinth you used to lounge against, back
when you were still smoking Marlboros & worried
you'd come to resemble your father, not yourself.

Subhash Jaireth
Brother Anton and Masha

'He has asked me
to marry him,'
Masha came and announced
seeking some response
support or perhaps consent.

He was standing
in the 'yellow' room
in front of the wide window
looking at a horse
rolling and revelling in the green grass.

'I have been asked
to marry him,'
Masha said again,
but the words after reaching him
collapsed like sounds without ripples.

He moved away from the window
took a few steps towards the table
picked up a half-written page
corrected a word, then two and
before the fourth word
ink on the tip of the pen dried
and he dropped the pen,

removed his pince-nez
coughed mildly, spat and
folded the blood-stained handkerchief
and turned to the window again.

The horse was up on its legs
and on the back of that brown horse
there was a golden bird whipping its tail.

'Masha,'
he said and turned
knowing that she was no longer there.

Across the corridor
there was Masha's room—
a narrow wooden bed
two vases with dried flowers
and a tall Anton looking down
from the sky-blue wall.

After a few days
they met again
walked through the forest
hunting for mushrooms
talked silently, smiled, occasionally laughed.

They were
the same brother and sister once again.

Komninos

It's Great to be Mates with a Koori

it's great to be mates with a koori
to know a gay man or two.
to have five lesbians for dinner,
and to cook them a vegetable stew.

it's a-m-a-z-i-n-g to have your chart done,
consult the tarot and the i ching.
to have a therapeutic massage,
and give the naturopath a ring.

it's sound to be found at a rally,
waving banners and shouting abuse,
at the c.i.a.'s involvement,
in wars and military coups.

it's hip to sip coffee at rhumba's,
whilst having an artistic chat.
drink pots and pots
of earl grey,
at baker's or the black cat.

it's grouse to pronounce spanakopita
the way the greek people do.
make humus at home in the blender,
tsatsiki and babaganouge.

it's great to relate as a person,
and not as a woman or man.

how dare you assume i'm heterosexual,
and hug friends as hard as you can.

but who do you see in the mirror,
when there's only yourself and you.
and who really knows the truth,
of the fascist, that lives inside, you.

Philip Salom

Benchleys (I)

Others say of Benchleys: no fools like old fools
worse two in one bed   breeding too late for decency
can you imagine them at it!   something erotic about the
   deformed
even then he was senile   that woman, more fool she
that hump!   always falling, skirt riding up her leg
its genetic   there should be a law
that stooped boy   that other, she thinks he's pure
that lout, surely, she   she's blind as a bat
there's more than one thing I'd say he did   he'll come unstuck
mark my words, to see   young and old mothers their faces
like fingers tightened back to the quick
the endless pain to raise just one more bewildered human.
As if time or accident, blood or worry
didn't break us down.
Here the tongue's slow targets: the loutish son
drives a colour-beaten vehicle, leans
his ugliness upon the sill. There is beauty in this.
Benchley smiles, hand on the top wire. His pigs
chew vacantly in the sun. There is beauty in this.
She picks gooseberries into her skirt, exposes
it just a little, a lumpish leg. There is beauty in this.
Not enough abject to pay off pity.
Not enough abject, the colour-beaten vehicles
of the heart. The deformed
are hardest to live with.

Train Talk: The Three of Us

Deep and roundish in the belly and because
she wore a bloomy dress I thought
her pregnant. She told me her husband
died wringing the arms of his lounge-chair
like a boxer trying to keep up close
and hanging on. It came just as she
knew it would. He'd chosen her she
said, to care for him until it did.
Gone. And no children. Miscarriage first
she said, and then—never. She
an Indian woman, never Oh Calcutta,
all the millions she was born among.
Her tone flat as the Nullarbor passing
and the days she must assess alone.
Outside, the horizon like an unmoved
yellow flame, the later bushes bursting.
Never, she said again. Her resignation
said courage, liberation.
A man who sat with us had stared
as she told me this, and all the time
he seemed about to cry. She said
I was kind and understood, but all
I did was listen. But now the air
took us, deep, roundish, she who
started this and then this man,
telling us his wife couldn't have a—
but he, his lips…oh the train was slow…
was desperate for a child. No, he kept
insisting he'd never leave her, never.
And myself, the father of a chosen *one*.
The air on us like air behind a train's
last carriage, eddying above the line,
uterine, like the ghost of a baby.

Nicolette Stasko
Keepers

They must still be around somewhere, those old things.
C.P. Cavafy, 'The Afternoon Sun'

Another birthday
card from my sister
nine days late
I rescue it from
the rain-soaked box
on the envelope
a customs slip
I misread 'pen'
for 'pin'   then feel the
lump with my fingers and all
my years
this moment's utter loneliness
inside
a cheap brooch   red and gilt
ballet slippers
slightly chipped
and I whirl
back eons to
my dancing days
when I was eight or seven
and dancing
was everything
the shock is like
a blow to the head
or the wind knocked
out
I breathe deeply
and read
in my sister's curlicue hand

'Remember this?'
It's not
the first time
she's done it
given me back what was mine
I can't figure out
where they come from
how she conjures
them up out of boxes or air
or dust
is it possible
my mother has succumbed
at last   mistaken
her daughters completely
and given the wrong one
the other's past?

and now my sister
feeds it drop by drop
transoceans
back to me

Louise Wakeling
The Water and the Wine
A Poem for the New Year

sing levy dew
sing levy dew
the water and the wine
the seven bright gold
wires, and the
bugles that do shine

Sing reign of Fair Maid
with gold upon her chin
Open you the East Door
and turn the New Year in

what's there to celebrate, we say
celebrating anyway
the raw beginnings of yet another year
in Paradise
the baby staggering on new legs
like a drunk
among the fluted martini glasses

this year we're painting the house red
what a night what a moon
what a world
time to hit the champagne
the chilli prawns
pan-fried in butter
take refuge in each other
and the brand-new video recorder

its black box lurks all day
on the lounge-room floor
like a resolution
waiting to be broken
(this year crims add us to their hit-list
midnight burglars will be drawn
like ants to our down-pipes)

hours later   John Cleese
lying in a ditch
in Norfolk   hopelessly late
for his moment of glory
tells himself he *does* mind   he *does*

now rain falls softly
where the tree-ferns arch their throats
and drink this New Year's water
once the Flower of the Well

the streets are strangely silent
before the neighbourhood count-down
10-9-8-7-6-5-4-3-2-1

somewhere in Fyall Street
a bagpipe wheezes into Auld Lang Syne

the heels of a later reveller
strike flint off bitumen
'Leave me alone will you
just leave me alone'
while the soft rain goes on falling

Stephen Edgar
Family Portrait

The sons and daughters are crossing to the island.
They've a duty to perform. Braving
The nets of spray, they keep to the deck,
The four of them, where luckily the wind
Makes talk impossible.
That's something that needs saving.

One of them has brought her smallest child,
An imp among trolls, who scampers
On the tightrope of their tacit mood
With mischievous balance. Cold
Is bluing her bare feet
But doesn't touch her. They freeze, for all their jumpers.

The empty cottage gives onto the bay.
The painted cat, coped
With smoke, still warms the fire. They feel
Like trespassers under a knowing eye.
They've come to pour their mother's
Ashes, as she'd wished, by her favourite eucalypt,

Yielding to ritual all failed expression.
They watch the box tilt
In the eldest's hands, and like a magic coffer
That can read a wish and fashion
It into a golden gift, this one
Works their various griefs to guilt.

He thinks, 'No one is responsible for ever.
Gratitude can't equal its demands.'
The second, 'Nothing one does fails
To hurt. We wear behaviour
Like a shirt of Nessus; loving
Or begrudged, in the end it all burns

To a remorse.' From the third the old complaint:
'We didn't ask to live. To have survived
Is a trick to put *us* in the wrong.'
The last, 'What is this contingent
Tie of blood? We might
Have been anyone. How should I have loved?'

They mumble some solemnities, awkward but earnest,
As the ashes are tipped out
Among coarse grass and strands of bark,
More like chips of bone than the dust
They'd thought wind might dispose of.
The dead aren't as obliging as all that.

Strangely, a picture seems appropriate.
So they huddle shivering by the bole
While a spouse takes aim. And the child
Asks, 'Will grandma be in it?'
They shudder. 'No dear.
Grandma's dead.' But they know she will.

Robert Harris

Forests & Rivers

I have this news: my niece has,
on the South Coast of NSW,
feet slipping on glassy earth,
chained herself, paused, shut
the padlock, stood beside
her chosen tree, eyed
dispute's shrill circle,

adjusted her footing,
thrown away the key.
From Redfern they bus in
more tactful police
to stand between them and the logging towns;
remand's six hours standing in the rain,
remand's this badge of protest,
this name Green. I know
the attitudes spring up like staves—
say a word at once
for the jouncing operators
coolly shifting the sticks and moving
tonnes! Can't you even drown
among some proper lilies?
asks the collective voice of supplements.
So soon, I've thought, to the fault line,
off to the gun-line in the long
anglic quarrel, so quickly to find
that class retaliation's darts
are cleverly, all-weather feathered
while betrayal walks in a press release
made of too ready assent on stilts
and the hundred obtuse arguments
spray flechets forward into future years.
Actually, I'm dismayed that this should happen.
Another life vexed
by the grudging sides.

Actually, I'm disturbed to find how proud.
It wishes not to be uttered and won't be silent.

Susan Hawthorne
Shell

My mother and I walk the back lanes of St Kilda
one sunny day in late October. Ghostly forms
like memories dart around us. This hotel,

where my grandmother lived throughout my childhood,
burnt down last year. Once grand it is now a shell.
From the lane I can see bathroom tiles dropping sheer

to the ground. My mother says, 'The two Miss Hawthornes
lived on that side,' pointing to the edge that wings back
towards where we stand. 'And Mill?' I say (for that's

what we called her) 'did she live at the front?' 'Mostly,
yes.' 'For how long?' My mother counts the years,
dropping out those not spent here. 'About seven, altogether.'

'I remember my fifth birthday,' I say, 'the cane cradle
Auntie Aldyth gave me.' And we came again when Mill
returned from England. It was the front suite, had one room

with a large oak table, another where she slept. She brought
dolls, and I, as the youngest, had to choose first.
My biggest responsibility to date. I picked the one

with the prettiest dress. Later, as I grew older,
I thought my sister's doll prettier. But on that day,
I was happy. Mill never left The Majestic. She died

in Fitzroy Street, hit by a tram. She's still there.
I see her sometimes, wearing faded purple dresses
of grandmother hue, soft like irises. And I know that underneath

is a whalebone corset so huge, it would take three of me.
We buy a strawberry gelato at Joes, and I am remembering
the pink flesh, the pink fabric that spread between the hard
     ribs of

Jonah's refuge. A link, perhaps, with my grandfather still
at sea. Today the tramlines stretch toward the sea,
and a hotel, once majestic, is a blackened shell.

Jill Jones
The Tax Form

It is a form of death, itemising
the half-truth of your life, a year—
or more if the phobia of forms gets you,
paralysed by boxes and instructions.
Troubling yourself, have you filled in
each gap so they won't catch
that whiff of fear—*please sir,*
think of my children, my house.
Is my address correct, do I really live
behind this door? There's a knocking,
a bulking uniform with a clipboard.
But it isn't possible, I don't even
drive a car.

                    Sorry, a mistake, it's
the Salvation Army rattling cans,
playing huge brass instruments—
do you remember on Christmas Day,
making carols sound mournful
at the street corner, presents inside
swimming in a tide of vivid wrapping,
bonhomie and kiddy greed?

This year try not to die, free
from your head's private lies
the truth about money. It resists
snug rationalisations, your secret reply:
please spend it on trees, and,
tear up the forms!
Hypocrite auteur—mon semblable.
You write, you read, papering life.
You freeze when you have to add it up.

Jean Kent
A Platform for Legends

On the verandah of my grandparents' house,
the day falls asleep around me.
This is the roof of my childhood.
And this, the floor. Tin and wood:
silver-grey, sibling corrugations.
Like platforms for family legends
they wait, rehearsing allegories
as if it is always the end
of a sun-limp day, the lucerne cut,
wheat bagged and a needle in the hessian
beckoning its tail of string.

In the fragrant dusk, soil settles.
Crickets, ants and unseen lives
team over cracks in black earth's surface—
years are strung like tales of Min-Min lights
along this world of roof-creaks,
board-sighs, a home paddock barracking
for the far-off calls of dinner plates,
falling tablecloths, cutlery and relatives.

Time melts here. Ghosts with glasses of Scotch
catching the last day's light in their hands,
bend their knees, ease back
into squatters' chairs. I wake.
A cool breeze is balancing
beside the verandah rail, roping it
and ruffling off, up into wisteria leaves:
sitting tenants now, under the roof.
Time melts. On the ends of long wooden arms,
ice, moonlit, hugs the air.

πO

The Women

The mother
waits outside the shop (after
church) and sends her son
inside
to fetch his
father.

The kid
rushs in (across
the floor) thru the smoke.
Up to his dad
who's playing cards;
Tugs at his sleeve and whispers (in
Greek): *Mum's outside.*
She says
to come down-
stairs.

Everyone
at the table asks
him if that's his son.
He says: *Yes,*
And deals another card.
'*Na s-e zisi*' they say.

The prostitute
nearby
smiles a warm: *Hello*
but the kid
gets scared; turns away and hides
his face.

Everyone laughs.

She *un-*
crosses her legs. Gets Up.
Straightens her dress;

And puts on another record;
As tho
she's forgotten all
about him
already.

Lyndon Walker
Dinner

They are a thin family
And their anger eats at them inwardly.
Strangely they don't keep pets,
Nothing that eats.

They appreciate photography
As a civilised form of art.
The layers of grey slide off one another
Fall softly to the carpeted floor
The surfaces shiny
The juxtaposition smooth.

There is a tension
In the polished air
When they sit with grace
Around the table.
It's a killing of the youth beast
And an exquisite form of torture.
It's like being forced to listen
To a concert of people starving.

John Foulcher
Pictures from the War

In 1945, on V-Day, my parents
first met. I still have the pictures: Dad in his slouch hat
and uniform, his arm linked through hers
like a finger clasping a trigger. Behind them,

balloons and streamers,
the prison gates of war
thrown open, the whole world granted amnesty.
They stare at the camera, clutched
in their instant of surrender, oblivious, crisp and new
in the sepia streets.
I think of them,
looking at these photos
of Hiroshima and Nagasaki.
In these pictures, a woman holds the charred barrel of her child,
while another fizzes with burns. Even in monotone,
blood has its own shade.
The city centre—
no people, only trees thin and black as electrical wire,
and outcrops of brick
jagging the pulped streets and parks. Everything over-exposed
in the flat expanse
of wedding-white light.

Skies

My father
was a draughtsman.
He died at night, slipped quietly
from a grid
of hospital corridors and beds.
In the morning, my brother and I knew nothing,
wandered about in the yard,
another day flexing
around us, while our aunts shadowed the house.
A steel blue sky
was scraping across the roofs
and powerlines. It was August (*that* month,
my mother called it
later). As she lay under the weight
of a tired winter,
the bedclothes slung about, her first words were:
'Your father, God took him'.

She'd had hours
to think of that. I remember the nylon curtains,
thin as mist,
and, through the venetian blinds,
slim blue lines of faultless, evanescent day.

In the time that followed, I often felt
the sky's pressure—
its clean, polished surface,
its edges, its extent;
there was always relief in cloud or rain,
anything to blur
the cruel line of the sun, drawn so sharply
across that day. Always, the sense
of other people's happiness
as light began to spill and glisten,
the sheer grey cloud
stretching and laddering...

Since then,
they've been particular skies,
wrapped over days
impossible to remember, or forget.
The morning our son was born,
for instance: night withering on the hospital glass,
the building's sharp black wings
shimmering with windows.
As I strolled to the car,
the leaves above me
were like schools of fish in a harbour of wind;
I was walking away from him,
going home
to sleep through the day.
Or the sky over sea
on a burnt afternoon
when he was four. I lay in numbing sunlight,
while he stumbled and shrank
into the tide,

clutching the yellow sky
of his kickboard; almost too late, a sliver of his voice...
my feet ripped open by rocks,
I held him,
sat breathless
and watched the sand become red as a sunset
in the places where I'd trod,
the sky rolling over me.

When my night comes, let me cut the sky free
and fold it away
like an architect's plan
for a house that nobody built. Let me have only
the darkness beyond,
filled with stars and sudden galaxies.

Myron Lysenko
Pets & Death & Indoor Plants

We're becoming old enough
to want to change our life-styles;
we're looking for substitutes
for sex & drugs and rock & roll.

But our dog...died
our cat...collapsed
budgies...wouldn't...budge.
Our roses...sank
our ferns...fizzled
cactus...carked it.

Yet, seated around roast dinners
our parents still talk about
the possibility of grandchildren.

Our minds...boggle
our bodies...fidget
our voices...falter.

We're still immature
& we'd like to be
for a few years yet.

The world's not ready for our baby;
we're not ready for the world.
We're still trying to learn

how to make love properly;
still trying to come to terms
with pets & death & indoor plants.

Tom Petsinis
From *Inheritance*

There's no past in dialogue—
we speak in the present tense
even in recollecting.
Summoning that girl again,
she approaches, steps on each
syllable, waves a ribbon
bartered from the gypsy wind.

A harbinger, with daisies
smiling from ankles and wrists,
and barefoot in the body
of the word, you skip toward
your grandmother sitting on
the kitchen step, murmuring,
stripping corn, filling her lap.

'Where are our stars, grandmother?'
'Child, they're too small to be seen.'
'Whose are they embroidered there?'
'They belong to the wealthy.'
'Will I ever own a star?'
'Silly child—it's time for sleep:
Our riches lie in our dreams.'

Crying, hungry, exhausted,
drawn by an older sister
who, gripping your fingers white,
threatens to leave you behind—
you glance over your shoulder
at homes dissolving in tears,
disappearing in smoke.

'Mother knocks, begging for bread.
We cling to her apron-strings.
A woman pledges some, but
when we've filled her water jugs
curses snarls at us instead.
I've forgotten many truths
since then, but that lie still hurts.'

Your father arises from
the still pond of your pupils:
solemn, he chants on Sundays,
at baptisms, burials,
and leaves in Monday's mist
with bullets crossed on his chest
to attack the Ottoman.

Last of a generation,
you're the way to beginnings.
As though worn by memory
the vein in your right temple
twists, takes me to a place
without trace in paint or print,
without a name on a map.

Kevin Hart

The Map

The maps of death get better every day—
Young draftsmen use a scale of one to one
With instruments that speed across a page.

So there's no need to hang around old graves
In black jeans, looking for a shady deal—
A simple map will tell you all you want.

You'll find a dozen in your corner shop.
I've heard it takes two trees to make each map,
Upsetting the environment, they say,

But people barely wait until they're home,
Unfolding sections on their lounge-room floor.
'Now where's the legend?' Father thinks aloud,

'Until we find the legend,' he expands,
'We can't tell if it's right-side up or not.'
It spreads into the kitchen, covers beds,

Then flaps out on the mail-box and the lawn...
Its creases are as sharp as Father's shirt.
'Beats me,' says Father, taking up his pipe

And rattling small change as he walks away.
'There's Uncle Harold!' Mother points, then goes
To make some coffee while the children stare

And play at generals, sticking in small flags.
'We'd best put it away now,' Mother says,
'Before Grandfather comes to see the kids.'

But already they've forgotten how it folds;
They try this way, then that. The map is vast
And all the neighbours help, but it won't close.

Peniel

Someone is whispering my name tonight.
Not here, although a radio sings the Blues
So softly you could almost hear a breath;

Not here, where moonlight chills the lemon tree
And makes a warmth out of the simplest touch.
My mother is dead: I have no name, and so

She quietly sings to me all day all night,
A name I never heard till now, a name
She whispered months before I was born.

My name is quiet as a fingerprint—
It makes no trouble, it tells me who I am,
I've seen it often. And yet, I don't know why,

These past few months I brood on Genesis,
Those stories like a rainbow at evening,
And find them all too true. At thirty-five,

All those I love have passed by Peniel,
And everyone longs to take another name,
And everyone knows a blessing is a wound,

And yet, what help is that? I do not know;
Those stories tell me nothing but themselves:
At three a.m. I find myself asleep

Beside some tales I hardly half-believe,
And doze again, as hearing my name sung,
A name no one has ever called me by,

Half me and half a child I never was—
My mother's child.
                    I wake sometime round four
And find the moonlight sleeping on my cheek.

'L'intelligence avec l'ange'
FOR ROBERT ADAMSON

I get up earlier these days, and leave
The house in darkness, scooping up my child
With mother's milk still clinging to her chin,
So that my wife can sleep. It is just light

In Princes Park, and Sarah is asleep
Just like her mother, now a mile away.
Before I left I let my fingers stray
Around my books, not turning on the light:

Now, sitting on a bench, I see the dark
Has given me *Feuillets d'Hypnos*. Yes,
A fine edition with pages roughly cut.
No one around: my mouth curves round those notes

Char scribbled on the run, inflamed by war,
And I translate one for my sleeping child—
'The fruit is blind. It is the tree that sees'—
Because she likes to look up at the leaves,

Then read again the one I know by heart,
About an angel living deep inside
That speaks the highest silence that there is.
I stumbled through a moment left ajar

And stayed two hours. Now Sarah rubs her eyes,
I drink some icy water from a tap,
And walk back home beside the Cemetery.
Your new poems flew here while I was out:

Both speak 'a meaning that we cannot count'.
I read them out aloud while Sarah feeds
And help myself to coffee, warm white rolls
And the dark honey that teaches us to sing.

Dorothy Porter
From *Akhenaten*
My Mother

My mother is a politician

and a good one

she loves power
she loves paper-work

that edge
that knot in her lip
    can send a scribe

or general
   to the pot
      with a griping gut!

my father plays
   in his inoffensive way
with his health
   or his harem

Mummy plays
   with gods
Mummy frightens
   iron.

My Daughter

'Daddy'
I stroked her arm
I sit up with Meketaten
my daughter
my quiet, shy girl
with a headache
   a sore throat
I hold her hand
'Daddy'
I'm here
she touches my face
it doesn't repel
   or enchant her
she just knows me
I'm her father—

'Daddy'
is she feeling well enough
   for this?
Nefertiti says no
   says she's too young
   calls me evil
   like Sobek

snapping off young legs
innocently fishing
in the swamp

I'm not the crocodile god
I'm of the Sun

I don't feed in dirty water
I love her
she's well enough
I take her in my arms
she trusts me
it hurts, she shivers
I stroke her face
'Daddy'

this is for the best
for my kingdom
I have six daughters
where else can I lay
my seed?
My daughter
my quiet, shy girl
goes to sleep
in her Daddy's arms.

I was quick.
Nefertiti
sulks in her rooms.

My Sleeping Brother

Asleep
Smenkhkare is cool.
And more fragrant
than melting scented wax.

I lean over him
and trail my hands
in his ripples.

But perhaps
I should stick to the safer lakes
    of Maru-Aten;
nothing is more dangerous
        for me
than swimming
    in the breath
of my sleeping brother.

Adrian Caesar
'Mamma's Cake'
(from an Italian recipe)

The day before leaving
I concoct three spongy tiers
for your birthday;
coffee, brandy, Tia Maria,
and mocha, melted velvet,

become exotic ingredients
of a layered grief,
to be plastered with custard
stirred for what seems like hours.
It threatens lumps as I fill up

with more than cognac
you help me strain the clotted mass,
clean the mess
I've splattered on the floor
restoring order until

the after dinner ritual:
cutting the cake of sentiment
it lies before us rich and cloying
promising indigestion.
'Too much will make you sick',

the old parental warning
echoes now as I remember

your keening face crumble
as you tried to say goodbye.

When I was a child you used to say
that I was good enough to eat,
but all I give you now
is this pathetic confection
piped with irony

too rich, not rich enough
for your loving hunger.

Graeme Dixon
To Let

Nice flat to let
the rental notice said
that's partly furnished
with large double bed
scenic ocean views
in a small quiet block
close to the port
near the south dock

I give it a ring
in the early morn
we needed a place
before baby was born
'come over and view'
the caretaker said
so I got the Mrs
out of mum's bed

'A home of our own'
she blissfully sighed
'I dearly wish
no one else has applied'
'Don't worry sweetheart'
I said confident

'I've got a good job
to settle the rent'

As soon as he saw us
it showed in his eyes
the critical look
the sarcastic sigh
'I'm sorry mate'
he said with a smirk
'we only rent
to those who work'

'I am employed!'
I answered frustrated
'and the finance companies
have me highly rated'
'That's not the point'
he said without tact
'the real problem is
we don't let to Blacks!'

So I hit him hard
on his fat chin
I was sick to death
of blatant racism
'Why don't they say'
I asked my wife why
'in the rental pages
Blacks need not apply'

But now I've found
a room of my own
The worry is
my wife is alone
in a women's refuge
I hope she is well
and as safe as me
in my prison cell

Jennifer Harrison
Swan Lake

Swan Lake ablaze with prawning lanterns.
My father drags the longest
and strongest until his net is full.
Women in their place on the bank
with the filleting knifes and the baskets
kids somewhere in the shallows
caught between androgyny and driftwood.
The wind rises. Peter is bitten by a fortesque.
The sandflies are silent.
My father drags again through the weeds.
I will be manly, waiting for him
until everyone's gone with their buckets.
I'll carry the other side of his net
through the middened darkness.
Help me sprinkle the catch with salt
he'll say—but I won't look
at prawns blushing, hissing in a pot.
I'll never eat prawns again
their shells like empty cupboards
stink of dead cats.

But as he eats the sweet meat
of the sea with lemon
I watch my father's arms rest on the table
then sleep in stringless nets
which haul and fish and let me go.

Peter Rose
The Living Archive
FOR MY MOTHER

Unwrapping a pair of luxurious towels—
one so dark as to be almost black,
the salesman quipped, stroking it
and his permanent wave, marvelling

at my tangible cash, the other
vaguely ruby for an anniversary—
unfolding these and holding up the
marked-down clock bought that morning
in a jeweller's shop half sealed off,
as if pearl and choker no longer paid,
you answered our facetious question
rather earnestly, which was unexpected,
saying you couldn't recollect unmarried life,
the twenty-odd years romanticized by a
fantastical son: waitress, stenographer,
the stoic girl outbraving rheumatic fever
(not once complaining, an uncle said),
one of Mario's dark-haired croonettes,
advised to concentrate on opera by a
visiting Italian tenor, but already
contracted to a bantamweight from the bush.
I have files on you, and fingerprints,
and photographs, yet the shards of memory
disintegrate under our feet—
leave me sentimental and otiose,
Antonia's archivist in the Offenbach,
the last romantic to convert to disk.
By then it was time for a toast,
my father and brother with their sudsy beer, ·
the two of us sipping nostalgic sherry,
as if the decades hadn't materialized
and a different dog wriggled on the rug.
Later, at the restaurant, for entrée
you served up familial anecdotage
(not your traditional fare): tales of
Robert's lethal cocktail, tripping
over snakes in the Warby Ranges,
our first morning in Auckland
when a bus missed me by that much.
If I knew this I had forgotten.
And what to do with a two year old's

first foreign foolhardiness,
often re-enacted on conscious kerbs?
Then the joke was on the guests,
all our respective anniversaries.
Around the table we went in a divorcing wave,
none outlustring the unimaginable ruby.
Like Donne's computing lovers
I stall at the first, and vainly project.
Chuckling at his end of the table,
the best my brother could do was three,
which we christened the Tinfoil Anniversary.

Judith Beveridge
Child Fishing

I

He holds a green nylon line around a cork core:
the weight of the apple he half eats.
Beside him, his father's reel races like a stopwatch,
clicks over, turns silent in the sea's lining of lead.
He casts into the spray, the driftwood.
Weed searches the ocean for its lost grip.

He hears his father curse the fish.
The rod almost doubles over, the sea
moans in its shells, its spiralled headphones
and the beach fills with the frenzy
of the winding reel. Along the clean gashes of gills
fish are lifted into names and gravity. A boy, he wanted

them loose and light as the moving, sinking kites
he casually held a string to. But his father
pulls them in, stiff as trophies, pulling at
the barbed clefs in their mouths and in a sleet
of fishscales cleans them, unstitching their intestines
with an intricate haberdashery of hooks.

II

In the wind a few scales carry. The boy catches
their scattered jewels. But the necessary gadgets
give death a stainless setting. Will his father
pass him the pocket knife, will his hands feel colder
than the threadbare weather when he incises
the fishes' gills and their greasy, satinette skins?

Lost green weed surges through the waves
as his father casts in. Sinkers
are like birthstones for the dead.
He wants to go home. It is dark. He watches the sea
glide under a polished deck of moonlight, the tide fill out
with light and a wave turn along precise pleats.

III

He feels something sinking into his life;
feels a storm's ready-sinkered lines;
feels his voice wasting in air like a gill.
In water, he sees himself as the discarded snarl
languishing towards the surface.
His line quakes like a handrail. He waits

for the first sounds on the surface
but hears only the reel ticking.
He dreams of the voice of his father
like a soft towel patted on his shivering skin.
But hears him cursing the fish, saying names
on his rosary of hook and gut, scraping the knife.

IV

Against a dark sea, he knows he can be taken
by a single cord and let drift. He knows no reel
stops at the shore. He looks at his father—

a weight he no longer feels buoyed to.
Weightless against a dark sea, he wonders when
he will be taken by a single cord and let drift.

V

He would like to thread scales onto a hook and slide
them up onto his line, like a trinket,
to colour them like sequins, a craft of buttons,
a charm against the reel's anti-chanting
and to wait for a tug on his line
to unravel him from the shore, past cuttlebone
dumped like sea plaster, past driftwood
and the weed washed up, to lift him into the white
rubble of spray and out to depths hitched under coral.
A dream his father would curse him for
as he stands with the half-bitten apple in his hands
and the lines are heavy, toyless kites

in a sunken sky that can jewel the light,
make a boy afraid. He knows the reel
can pulverise his jewels to grit as he stares
at the beach, the ground lockets of shells
that once held his portrait. He knows
he can no longer be buoyed to his innocence,

to the bell of his heart against danger.
He knows his father will hand him the trophy
of the knife and the reel to be worn at the wrist:
an amulet with which to blaspheme at the tides.
He knows he will let the souls of fish
fly from their gills, that he will scrape the knife

along the shields of their sides and his father
will look towards the sea with a blessing.

Sherryl Clark
Things That Change Us

The day she came home
after three years overseas
cracked our solid family in two.
No smiles, only tears and
a crazed hurt from betrayal that splattered
acid over anyone who came too close.
Mum and Dad were helpless,
unable to withdraw, incapable
of understanding where the edge was.
She lashed out,
cut deep and couldn't see our pain
beyond her own.
Even I, adoring but unwary at eleven,
did not escape.
I'd put my sister on a pedestal
and then she jumped—
for her it was only a step,
for me it was the height of a cliff
and the smash when she hit the ground
beside me, still echoes through my life.

S. K. Kelen
The House Spider

The spider was there when we moved in
basking on a sunlit bit of wall
waving its front legs in greeting.
Dad said it was 'a cheeky bastard'
then, checking his language &
waxing more lyrical, called
the huntsman 'an eight-legged fox'.
Dad put the spider outside
catching it gently in a glass spider jar
& letting it loose in the backyard.

But it kept coming back, that cheeky
eight-legged bastard. (Calling a spider
a fox cut no ice with us.) And Dad kept catching
him in the spider jar & tossing him
into the backyard, saying 'he should be outside
hunting rats & taking his chances with the cat.
Out you go, quick smart.'
For weeks this went on, Dad with excuses like
spiders belong under rocks or what if
it scares the kids. But we weren't scared.

'Huntsmen should be out hunting' Dad announced
catching the poor cheeky bastard by surprise
in the spider jar and letting him outside.
But that night, after Dad had been smoking, the
spider was back inhaling the blue air.
The cheeky bastard beckoned with his front legs
'follow me' and demonstrated the webbed traps
'round the house with trapped flies, moths & mozzies
—an impressive bounty.

From that day on, they were great mates.
Dad'd stay up late reading & writing
& the spider would appear on the door-frame
to relax or flamboyantly hunt moths
buzzing the light
& sometimes sat next to Dad
on the arm of his comfortable chair.

Then one day Dad found the spider
half-dead with three legs missing
under a toy car. I can't say who did it.
The cat had sneaked in the night before.
(The cat was never allowed in.)
I mean the privileges accorded that cheeky bastard
seemed a little undue: the run of the house
staying up late with Dad
reading, writing, having
fun.

Warwick Wynne
Tractor and Father and Child
For Liam

In the front yard
of a farmhouse
by a cooling tractor
a man is hugging his child.
See, these things can be connected;
the tractor, red and powerful,
oversized wheels like a boy's toy,
one of those that overturn regularly
on the sloped lands
in moments of imagination,
and the man and the child hugging.

There has been no family tragedy
no accident has drawn the man
from his fields in sullen grief.
He is not hugging the child
out of guilt or regret or sadness,
unless it is the inevitable sadness of the future.
They hug each other for a long moment
no indecision or unease between them
then the child is placed on the grass
and the tractor is driven away.
Nothing out of the ordinary has occurred.
In the west the day is ending.
Now they will go inside and eat dinner together.

Anthony Lawrence
The Drive

My father could not look at me
as we sat in the back of a white sedan
on our way to the police station.
But I looked at him. He was staring

straight ahead through all the years
his son had disappointed him.

News had come through of the boy
who'd fire-bombed the car outside
the Methodist Church. When the detectives
arrived, I was having a family
portrait taken. I saw the suits and ties
in the window, then the doorbell rang.

I smiled into the flash, ran to the bathroom
and vomited my head off. I wanted to make
the Australian team as a fast bowler.
I wanted Frances Clarke to love me.
But instead I'd struck a match and immolated
the minister's new Valiant, my breath

punched out of my lungs by the boom.
I ran behind the Sunday-school buildings
and confessed to the lawn-raking currawongs.
I watched black smoke like useless prayer
gutter into the Sydney sky.
The sirens were a long time coming.

As we pulled into the station carpark,
dead leaves and the two-way static
sounded like years of thrashings: blue
welts across the backs of my legs like
indelible neon, and my mother's weeping
for the times I nailed her with insults

to the wall. But now, after breakdowns,
divorce and a distance of eighteen years,
we can talk about the sound a belt makes
as it flies in the bathroom; about
the violent spirit of a teenage son.
My mother kisses my eyes to stop

the sadness we've known from breaking
through. My father tells me about his life

instead of brief reports from the office.
I love them, these parents and strangers,
these friends who appear from time to time,
sharing their names, their blood.

The Custodian of Grief and Wonder

She is the custodian of grief and wonder.
On Thursday she drove with her son
to the crematorium, where she read to him
from a small brass page in a wall
of many pages, then polished the solemn
poetry with her sleeve.
                              On Friday
her son wanted to know what happens
in the flames. She told him that fire
takes the body and frees the spirit,
and that ash is the breath of the dead.
On Saturday he placed the urn containing
his father's breath to his ear
and listened.
                    He was sure he heard him
laughing then—a grey laugh
rising from the breakers as he stood
on the sand. He saw his father consumed
by a rolling wave of fire, though
the laughter kept coming until it became
a gull's cry, wind in the headland grass…
And he turned the urn slowly in his hands,
listening for the voice of love: the tide-
drawn rattle of shells and stones?
The sound of his father surfacing?

Sarah Day
The Christening Dress Comes Airmail

Between Manchester and Melbourne
jetting a blue arc,

a brief scrawled address
and the tiny portrait

of an unblemished queen
its pinked frame of reference

among so many Christmas greetings,
single serves of Life-Long milk,

hundreds of turkey dinners
warming to the indefatigable

engine sound; above, a pilot murmuring
to time-lapsed sleeping listeners

in a prolonged indigo dawn
that India drifts somewhere down below,

the century-old cambric dress comes flying.
An infant form folded in brown paper,

silhouette of generations,
four indelible lives

the shape of children
roughly one age

intimate with one another's faces, blood,
each wearing, knowing the other, all the others.

Lionel Fogarty
The Mununjali Exemption Man
TO MY GREAT GRANDFATHER FRED FOGARTY

The Department of Family Services and Abos lied to me.
My grandfather came to Purga at 'bout 19 or 18 hundreds and
married a Murri woman who gave him sons. In 1922 he was
given exemption certificate from the acts. He came from
Mununjali people who lives in Beaudesert. My grandfather
was gammin and told he was free, but when his son hit the
manager his son was sended to Barambah.

Now my two grandfathers are dead and my parents can't remember any things they said or done cause in those days it was hard to tell.

So all I want to know is who was my great-great-great-grandfather's parents? Now some of these good christians must have paper records.

You see brothers and sisters I don't need whiteman papers to prove, but I want it to fight for legal—our land and cultural heritage rights.

Purga my grandparents help built, now is not ours. Well look at the mixed up mess.

Oh great grandfather I can't hear your yarning 'bout our relations Oh great grandfather I have your grandchildren ready to take up the fight for our land and losted you were taken and I'm lacking, so why don't we all come together as a family and re-issue free knowledge. Now my great grandfather was an aboriginal man dat is divide from me cos the history has changed camps. But I have moved too, yet I have a marriage certificate to you great-great-grandfather, and I will find you waiting in Mununjali Dreaming realities.

Paul Hetherington
Uncle Bible

Uncle Bible we called him as we grew:
he visited every second month or so
and brought strange habits; strange, stern words

pronounced in tones that mimicked kindliness
while eating scones and gulping strong dark tea,
and laughing once or twice uproariously

at nothing funny. No-one quite explained
his relationship to us, or why his words
were privileged above the family's.

He always had his stubborn small black book,
'*New Testament*', he said, 'that shows you kids
how to cleanse yourselves of filthy sin.'

At this my aunt seemed discomfited
but did not interrupt. His stares were clubs
heavy with portent, driving doubt in me

so deep I later lay distraught in bed
and felt his hell-fire ripple through my sin,
his awful words black leeches on my skin.

Stephen J. Williams
Flowers for the Dead

Ask me why I write so many poems about the dead
And I tell you it is because there are so many of them.
Ask me why these poems must be written and I tell you
It is because other poems are wrong and must be corrected.

What is wrong about these other poems? you want to know.
I heard one say, 'My friend, who is dead now, sat with me
All afternoon and there was nothing to say, and when I was
   leaving
He stopped to take a flower from his tree and gave it to me.'

I heard another say, 'Don't be sad—This is only as This is,
Things growing and things dying in their cycle, all
In their own time and in their own way dying. The dead
Are dead and gone. Life goes on. So, go.'

The purpose of a poem is to say what is—with the force
Of a hammer. When it comes down, this hammer, the poem
That comes with it, about that dead lover or that dead father,
Should strike you in the throat and make you speechless.

So, when someone has died, do not take flowers with you.
When it is your turn to write about the dead do not write
About flowers, or afternoons in the sun, or cycles, or God.
Tell it as it was. Get out your hammer and drive the nail in.

For example, the poem of a father says, 'He preferred
Pain to morphine, hiding pills the doctor gave because pain
Told him he was still alive. He died in a hospital bed.
His cleaning woman was standing beside him.

'Yes. That's right. *The cleaning woman.* Fearing love more
Than death, Daddy would not let the family know
He was human and in need of love. We read about it
In the classified columns of the daily newspaper.'

For example, the poem of a lover says, 'I thought—
Who the fuck is this man with bones sticking up under
The skin of his back, who looks jagged and cold as a lizard?
When you said you were hungry and I made dinner,

'I knew you were going to throw up, and you did
—In my lap. Thanks. Let's make a deal. I forgive you
For looking at me with those weightless, jealous eyes, if
You forgive me for hoping you would die more quickly.'

When someone has died, do not take flowers with you.
Make poems in the teeth of your grinding jaw and bursting
     head.
The dead don't need flowers or poems about flowers.
The dead leave pain behind them so we know we are still alive.

Philip Hodgins

Shooting the Dogs

There wasn't much else we could do
that final day on the farm.
We couldn't take them with us into town,
no one round the district needed them
and the new people had their own.
It was one of those things.

You sometimes hear of dogs
who know they're about to be put down
and who look up along the barrel of the rifle
into responsible eyes that never forget
that look and so on,
but our dogs didn't seem to have a clue.

They only stopped for a short while
to look at the Bedford stacked with furniture
not hay
and then cleared off towards the swamp,
plunging through the thick paspalum
noses up, like speedboats.

They weren't without their faults.
The young one liked to terrorise the chooks
and eat the eggs.
Whenever he started doing this
we'd let him have an egg full of chilli paste
and then the chooks would get some peace.

The old one's weakness was rolling in dead sheep.
Sometimes after this he'd sit outside
the kitchen window at dinner time.
The stink would hit us all at once
and we'd grimace like the young dog
discovering what was in the egg.

But basically they were pretty good.
They worked well and added life to the place.
I called them back enthusiastically
and got the old one as he bounded up
and then the young one as he shot off
for his life.

I buried them behind the tool shed.
It was one of the last things I did before
we left.
Each time the gravel slid off the shovel
it sounded like something
trying to hang on by its nails.

From *The Way Things Were*

Our footy ground was just behind the hall.
Its space reserved for playing out a myth
and its oval shape a homage to the ball.

The north-wing grandstand was a giant mouth
that roared refrains at umpires who couldn't see,
especially when the boys were on the meth,

although the place to hear the greatest poetry
was where the old blokes gathered near the scoreboard.
They had a grasp of metaphor and simile

that would have done the Martian poets proud,
and as for that device of bringing the past
into the present, they used it all they could.

Inside the clubroom were photos of the best
and fairest players, and teams that had won the flag.
And down the honour board there was a list,

divided into years, of players from the league
who served and died in World War One or Two.
Their stanzas looked like poems on the page.

The footy there was family. You knew
your team-mates as if they were next of kin,
and most of the opposing players too.

There was a whole complicated world within
those teams. You played for maybe twenty years
from midgets up to ones or twos and then

you had your name in all those two-tab free-verse
odes of names that came out each Thursday night
and told you which identity was yours

and who your brothers were. The men who wrote
those poems knew you like your parents did
and gave you lines that your parents could not.

Little Elegies

For children lost in accidents on farms
it's that much further for their parents' love.

Their grief, receding closer to their child,
begins with time and place, and random cause.

The fatal tractor grumbles down a lane
just like it did before the sway-bar slipped;

the shotgun leans off-duty in the shed,
its bright red cartridges like fallen fruit;

the dully sliding channel looks unmoved
by drama at the culvert yesterday;

and where the tiger-snake was killed too late
some tidy ants are picking meat from bones.

For those two people living with this death
the silent meals, the nights of lying still

are like it always is when they're apart.
At any time it seems that one of them

has stopped half-way through packing little clothes
into a box and stands there loose with tears

while in a distant paddock in the heat
the other one is shovelling out a drain,

becoming more and more obsessed with work:
as though they might as well have never met.

Richard J. Allen
From *What to Name Your Baby*
III   The Father

What if he's running an international spy ring in her belly?

What if he has gone undercover to escape from the bad guys?

What if he's hiding out from the good guys?

What if he's an alien life form that is controlling his mother's body?

What if he's part of the advance guard of an alien invasion force planning to take over the world?

What if that's why he's always sleepwalking his mother to the
   fax machine in the middle of the night?

What if that's why she presses pieces of blank paper to her belly
   and then sends the strangely vibrating pages down the mouth
   of the fax machine to numbers she's never heard of?

What if that's why she has strong cravings to swallow a portable
   telephone?

Catherine Bateson
Persephone's Visit

You've lost weight, twig-thin. You used to be plump
as a new peach and those shadows under your eyes.
You're sleeping alright? Black doesn't suit you.
Never did. What happened to that little yellow frock I sent?
When you were fourteen yellow was your favourite colour.
Black makes you look sallow and too skinny.
No man wants to hug bones at night
no matter what the ads say.
You're not dieting again?
There's no trouble between you two?
Not that you'd tell me if there was.
A mother learns to wait.
I remember when you were always smiling—
little sunflower your father called you.
I'm warning you, no husband wants to come home to frowns.
You'll get wrinkles. No-one ages faster
than a scowling woman.

She leaves as soon as she can.
Never remembers not to slam the screen door.
Every summer I promise myself
it will be different. We'll really talk.
Elbows on the kitchen table.
I'll ask what books she's read, is she still painting?
I'll show her the garden.

But I hear my voice—nag, nag, on and on.
She scares me, this grown-up
daughter. So reserved, so
polite. Yes, please
mother. No thank you
mother.
What can you do?
There's so little time.

When she leaves I go to my own mother's grave.
Forgive me, mother,
forgive me.

This is a Poem...

This is a poem written on the long afternoon
of a child's illness,
when each hour drags past with aching limbs.
It needs to be read accompanied by Frère Jacques
played again and again by a clockwork toy
and a radio must talk softly to itself in another room.

This poem will be interrupted by the child crying
the woman chanting mantras of comfort
a phone call to the doctor
another to her spouse or friend.

This poem will pause for three minutes
so a temperature can be taken
and there must be time in it to coax a child to feed.

This poem should be written on pale lilac paper
fading into grey
just as the child's eyes are shadowed and the afternoon
and the paper should be scented faintly
with the smell of rain
and fever.

At any time this poem may be abandoned
on a seat in Casualty

or by a bed on Seven West
and then you will have to finish it;
remembering how little a child weighs
in your arms
and how you can make your hands steady as a surgeon's
though fear storms your heart with cyclonic fury.

This poem ends in silence
so you may listen to the child breathing.

Jordie Albiston
Letter Home (Mary Talbot)

Mary Talbot was an Irishwoman convicted for stealing, who was transported to Sydney without her children. She wrote her letter during the voyage in 1791, and died soon after arriving in Sydney.

Most honoured Sir, since I was sentenced for
lifting the linen, I have not seen my children
except in my mind. Sir, I pine for their faces
and soft little arms, and as they fall ever further
behind, I beseech you to find them and, *aided
by God*, restore them to their mother in time.

I leapt into water from a Gravesend hulk but
was captured and sentenced to die. I then lay
a long day in the Newgate gaol (my death
delayed by the child inside) 'til the court did
decide transportation for life to the colony of
Botany Bay. Sir! I did want to die! My shrieks

echoed high as they replaced me to prison, my
whole body crying at what lay ahead, protesting
most strongly for the rope round my neck to
stifle my sore sense of reason. But my sentence
prevailed, and the *Mary Ann* sailed with my
children's mother aboard. If you could afford

further *generous exertions* on their behalf and
on mine, pray apply for my pardon and have me
returned to the other side of the Line. I thank
God for your goodness and all of your effort to
recall *your most humble servant*. And writing
my name, I remain the same: yours, *Mary Talbot*.

Lisa Bellear
Mother-in-Law

Took me thirty years before I left your father
Battered wife syndrome, well that's the term the
Social worker used at the neighbourhood centre
Oh I didn't realise I was being abused. On the bad days
I never left the house, told friends, not that I had many
I was visiting a relative who had taken poorly
Look at me sweetheart, you've made the right decision
Believe me, you have to think of Stacy, and don't forget
You have to take care of yourself. Mothers have rights
Mothers have needs too. I'll not make excuses for
Your behaviour, you have to work through that, nor
Can you say it was all Larry's fault. Honey don't cry
Together we'll be okay, you've got to stop hating yourself
Alright, the court order allows fortnightly access visits
On the proviso he's not been drinking—listen he's not
Doing right by you or Stacy, coming here drunk. He
Hasn't even bothered to shave. Darling, he may still care
He may even still love, but rules are there for the protection
Of the child, and for the sanity of the mother. Maybe the
Next time you will be able to welcome Larry inside but
For now, tonight, the situation, the reality is no, and if
He's still there in five minutes, Larry knows the score
There's a train, or there's a police van
It's up to him

Alison Croggon
From *Domestic Art*

1   Labour

pain grabbed me cruelly and tossed me
into the violent land of my body.
all around were ravines and crags
and the freefall of exhaustion.
the only way out was through. at the end
you split out of me like a ripe seed
and opened your unused eyes on my sweating skin.

2   Hymn

neither maid nor matchless
neither still nor blest
I woke with knowledge in my womb
and fear within my breast

the day was five hours old
when Joshua wriggled out
to check what all the dim reports
of noise were all about

he is a knot of needs
my ends are all astray
and the hours are short and fat
with Joshua in my day

3   Cooking

rise into me like new cake
bunched and sorry you loud snout
bursting your sheaf of blind
legs you lust of fists writing
all over me squiggles and
drizzles of must o my

juicy suckling out of the
oven and perfectly
crusted all over with smiles

John Kinsella
The Hay King's Recalcitrant Daughter

1

Of all he surveys least surveyed
is his recalcitrant daughter. The spread
of fields about the terraced hill
of his walled city state satisfies
his heart no longer, instead he follows
the sun's corridor and moon's tunnel
with only his daughter in mind. Hay balers
package the produce of his rich soils,
sheep move in orderly flocks through corridors
between the hay or over coarse tracts of stubble.
Windmills turn smoothly even in faint breezes.
Dams remain viable throughout summer
and his land is free of salt.

2

Jo-anne lives with Emily in Harvest Valley.
They don't grow their own food, nor keep animals.
They are not artists nor work in a bar. They
do not love but are fond of each other.
Jo-anne misses her father but doesn't mention
this to Emily who can't stand the red-faced farmer.
'He's a fascist,' she would say, whenever
the Hay King's name cropped up. Jo-anne always
agreed, even developing the theme, 'Yeh,
up there in his palace, master of servants
and peasantry, with himself and poisoned memories.'

Anathalamion

My parents dead & the family property
broken up, I live on *their* place—in the old shearing
quarters—& keep an eye on things. Talking
business with the old man is impossible though the old lady
comes to the quarters once a week & we sit with a cuppa &
    study
the week's takings—sorting out the bills & tallying
the red & black figures. She's always been good
with numbers. But it's like she's given up caring
about things really—just working the sums to trade
away the bad memories. The old man sits in a hide
down by the creek some days—watching the blue heron
high in the redgum tree that was blasted
by lightning years back. When I go to the hotel
they ask me what the old couple do these days but I just get
    plastered
& stare into my beer—snubbing even the mayor—'to Hell
with the lot of you!' I'll yell, just waiting for a quarrel.
On a dark day, when the season was closing in,
they were seen leaving the town, like the blue heron.

After their son's death the blue heron became the old man's
obsession and his wife told me he only ever spoke to her when
talking of them. The blue heron, their nest raided by crows,
have left the redgum this year. I like to think they're nesting
nearby—maybe further upcreek where the redgums are still
thick. Their son had once claimed that he'd been told by a
hay stooker that if you died near a heron your soul joined
with its soul. He'd told that to his parents and they'd laughed.
He marvelled that it was called a blue heron when it was more
of a grey colour. On a dark day, when the season was closing
in, they were seen leaving the town, like the blue heron.

As children we'd burrow into the hay
or move bales like building blocks, trapping
carpet snakes. Together saw Tad Hunter clutching

at the mangled stump of his arm, the auger crazy
with his blood. Once we nearly drowned in a silo of barley,
sinking further with every move, pulled out crying
by his old man who said we'd learnt our lesson & didn't need
punishing any further. Who said the same, when—riding
his motorbike—we hit the cattle grid & skewed
into the creek. And when we fed a pet sheep his premium seed
wheat & watched it die from pickle poisoning. Neighbours
called us feral kids—'little bastards, getting their claws
into everythin', like locusts in the crop, nothin' can stop
'em.' It's true, we ran amok, but we did our chores
& didn't mean any harm—a chip
off the ol' block his dad would say to the town cop.
On a dark day, when the season was closing in,
they were seen leaving the town, married again.

In some ways it was like a world under glass—porous glass that
let in the creek and the birds and the weather and the children
who'd creep up to the house as a dare, the old people having
that reputation for strangeness, but kept the pain in, petrified
in the moment. The boy's death had cut it off from the outside
world and it existed in a twilight which not even the most
determined seasons could breach. I never said much about him.
I read a lot and kept to myself. But even the brightest books
seemed dull. The shadows of the blue heron indelible on their
pages. On a dark day, when the season was closing in, they were
seen leaving the town, like the blue heron.

It was one of those days when the black
cockatoos were low-loping in a storm-stained sky
& the creek ran river-thick, scouring the red clay
banks & swamping the nests of water rats, & the track
up to the top gate was up to the axles with mud & a long trek
around the flooded paddocks was necessary, stray
sheep stuck firm, the silos damp & full of sprouted wheat,
that they both emerged in black raincoats & doggedly
made their way to town on foot. As word had spread, the main
    street

was lined with adults & children who thought they were in for
   a treat.
But the old couple didn't lift their heads, & neither led
the other as they marched like mourners or a parody of the
   dead,
marching a slow funereal slog towards the empty church.
A few moments later the priest appeared
& followed them into the silence beyond the arch.
On a dark day when the season was closing in,
they were seen leaving the town, married again.

Tracy Ryan
Morningswood

Playing with fire.
Dad lets me carry in
sticks and twigs for the kitchen
stove. *Morningswood*, he says.
Mum corrects him: *Kindling*.
Well, where I come from, Dad begins,
and it begins again.
I say nothing
never name
this stuff that sets it all alight.
That narrow mouth with its sliding grate
consumes all that's useless, does away
with cover-ups, old news, stale arguments
and in exchange
feeds and warms us. We take it for granted.
Buttering up the jaws
of the old jaffle-iron
we metamorphose
all last night's leftovers
smashed peas that slid round the plate
stiff remnants of potato mash
and hated carrots—
into a crisp toast-pocket that'd

sizzle the roof of your mouth off.
One way to make her eat veges at least—
says Mum—*but it's dangerous.*
Sitting this close to the source
my face is burning.

Later, bringing sticks in again
to fire up my own hearth
I dare the word
Morningswood.
My husband looks up
sees the hard logs give way
flames taking all the unsaid
we make bonfires of.

Exegesis

Her body is a palimpsest   was it ever virgin   bears
words like wounds   in shorthand   scar   on the left
foot   running after her mother to the river   a whole
winter she can't remember   sealed in there   shoulders
riddled with freckles   a secret code the heat brings out
that summer   at Rockingham   with her father   who
denies it   who denies her   body   layers peel off like
drafts or depositions   truths gone underground   to
stomach or womb   irretrievable

Coral Hull
White Linen at Midnight

my mother at midnight/ her slender waist/ her
wrists/ moving beneath the clothesline/ her naked
arms reaching/ into frozen white linen/

                             she is seen/
briefly between each billow of sheet/ & wind-lifted
pillow slip/ it is here she abandons me/ for the
soaking white linen/

                   frozen like starlight/ between

her fingers/ in the haze of pollution/ in the city
sky glowing/ i long for my mother/ her hands in
soapy water/ knuckle-bleached white/

                                she is untouched/
partially hidden/ within midnight breeze/ my mother
turning/ within folds of gently flapping linen/

in ripples like calm ocean/ or old blinds tossed/
by a cool change from the south/ her gaze faintly
chilling/

          her toes wedged in sandals/ crushing the
frosty lawn of our backyard/ i wish she would touch
me/ but she is only reaching higher into linen/

into cotton nappies/ white from scrubbing/ her
knuckles pink & raw/ from nights of endless rubbing/
in the industrial glow of the small laundry/

                                  i am
left in darkness/ cast by the shadow of her washing/
in the moon brightness/ of her vision extending
outwards/

         i am always on her outskirts/ wishing it
were my skin/ she were holding/ instead of clean
white linen/

             & my midnight father/ hot & drunk
behind her/ her skin pale white/ her mind starlit/
stretched into night beyond the yard/

                         galaxies apart
from his ravings/ waiting for the cold quiet
morning/ of linen bundled into her arms like empty
pillow cases/

            my thin white mother stretching into
linen/ her ankles long/ strapped into vinyl sandals/
tissue-soft her skin/ her throat exposed & white/
my father drunk/ abusive/ following her from the
bedroom/ to the kitchen/ to the laundry/ with the
vacuum/ the clothesbasket/ the dirty washing/

she pushed it across the carpet/ carried it/
scrubbed it clean/ folded it neatly/ placed it
inside the linen press/

                 the shadow of his anger/ &
hatred/ upon her naked white shoulder/ she thought
she was a fairy/ & him the ogre/

                     but his bitterness/
& self-loathing had weakened her/ she wanted to be
alone/ but he followed her/ everywhere/ to the same
clothesline/ for thirteen years/

                 white linen at
midnight/ my mother wrapped in it/ as inaccessible
as the light/ thrown down from stars/

                    as cold &
lovely as midnight frost/ smothering the lawn of
our backyard

Lucy Dougan
My Father in His Thornproof Jacket from Cavan

Imagine his two hands
crossed up to the neat flecked cuffs of olive.
They reach in gentle as feathers to part the overlay
of blackberry thorn and gorse, unscathed,
and there reveal a pristine clutch of speckle,
or wait (these are things we did not do).
Maybe a mote from his finespun jacket
tickles trout in the Blackwater River.
Remember, yes, a portly gentleman, belted
bespectacled, spotted with age—
motley…and didn't he once play Bottom?
Foolish, I wonder, wise, enchanted I
pull at gorse and thistle, torn,
unproofed by the landscape of his coat,

by things he might have taught me, camouflage;
the art of empathy.

He is gone from me now, safe across that fierce border of briar
and from his rood of blackthorn shoots my cover.

Jemal Sharah
The Lares

It dates back to the Etruscans, the custom
of household gods; before the tribes of our ancestors
overran Europe, each family
had its guardians. The Romans took it on;
and we, too, have our own: the dog.

Like the Latins', our lives are structured round him.
We invoke him on waking, on going to bed;
on leaving the house we also address him.
He is our conscience, our sense of responsibility:
it is he we go home to, he who hinders our holidays.

His needs persuade us out into the air
in winter's cold and summer's stickiness.
From each meal he takes his propitiation,
the last pieces from each dish. (In return
he barks all day at neighbours, passers-by.)

Dogs are the dumb chroniclers
of the familiar; like Lares, they remind of past events.
Ours saw out an owner's, my brother's, death;
our move from Canberra; and returned from abduction.
It is pets, not parents, shellshocked children cry for.

It wasn't accidental that the Lares
were always shown beside a dog—
'symbol of vigilance and fidelity'.
The Romans understood dogs—from the matron's pet
preserved in fresco, to carved stone hunting hounds,

or the mosaic in the entrance,
the ominous message, 'Beware of the Dog', belied
by the artist's rendition: the frisk
and mock-growling of the dog dancing around him,
its ecstatic wriggle of welcome.

Through history dogs have created normality
in art: the tail which disappears
beneath the last Supper's tablecloth, the pup
pressed to the knight's stone feet upon the tomb.
They are domestic gods—the humble, the ordinary.

Endlessly loyal, they're the ultimate innocents:
more dependent than a child, though their lives
are more separate. Yet dogs have style—
stretched in the sun, inspecting a flea, a paw,
they always rouse a smile.

SOURCES AND ACKNOWLEDGMENTS

The editor and publisher wish to thank copyright holders for granting permission to reproduce textual extracts. Sources are as follows:

Robert Adamson: 'My First Proper Girlfriend' from *Selected Poems 1970–1989*, University of Queensland Press, St Lucia, 1990; 'Fishing with My Stepson' from *The Clean Dark*, Paperbark Press, Sydney, 1989; 'The Australian Crawl' from *Waving to Hart Crane*, Angus & Robertson, Sydney, 1994. **Jordie Albiston**: 'Letter Home (Mary Talbot)' from *Botany Bay Documents*, Black Pepper, North Fitzroy, Vic., 1996. **Richard J. Allen**: 'The Father' from *What to Name Your Baby*, Paperbark Press in association with Tasdance, 1995. **Dorothy Auchterlonie**: 'Equation' from *The Dolphin*, Australian National University Press, Canberra, 1967. **Catherine Bateson**: 'Persephone's Visit' from *Pomegranates from the Underworld*, Pariah Press, Kew, Vic., 1990; 'This is a Poem . . .' from *Walking the Dogs* (ed. Mal Morgan), Pariah Press, Kew, Vic., 1994. **Eric Beach**: 'Hollowcourt Centre for Intellectually Disabled Adults', 'Once was Always', and 'A Scrapbook of Sun' from *Weeping for Lost Babylon*, Harper Collins/Angus & Robertson, Sydney, 1996. **Bruce Beaver**: 'Remembering Golden Bells …' and 'Letters to Live Poets X' from *New and Selected Poems 1960–1990*, University of Queensland Press, St Lucia, 1990. **Lisa Bellear**: 'Mother-in-law' from *Dreaming in Urban Areas*, University of Queensland Press, St Lucia, 1996. **Judith Beveridge**: 'Child Fishing' from *The Domesticity of Giraffes*, Black Lightning Press, Wentworth Falls, NSW, 1987. **John Blight**: 'Family Ties' and 'Houses and Homes' from *New City Poems*, Angus & Robertson, Sydney, 1980. **Norma Bloom**: 'The Inheritance' from *When I See You*, Cat & Fiddle Press, Hobart, 1978. **Margaret Bradstock**: 'Letter to My Daughter' from *Flight of Koalas*, Blackwattle Press, Sydney, 1993. **Christopher Brennan**: 'The Wanderer (94)' from *The Verse of Christopher Brennan* (ed. A.R. Chisholm), Angus & Robertson, Sydney, 1960. **Doris Brett**: 'From Snow White's

Stepmother' from *In the Constellation of the Crab*, Hale & Iremonger, Sydney, 1996. **Lily Brett**: 'Children I' and 'I Wear Your Face' from *The Auschwitz Poems*, Scribe, Brunswick, Vic., 1986. **R.F. Brissenden**: 'Building a Terrace' from *Building a Terrace*, Australian National University Press, Canberra, 1975. **Kevin Brophy**: 'Painting Session' from *Seeing Things*, Black Pepper Press, North Fitzroy, Vic., 1997. **Vincent Buckley**: 'Stroke' from *Arcady and Other Places*, Melbourne University Press, 1966. **Joanne Burns**: 'Australia' from *On a Clear Day*, University of Queensland Press, St Lucia, 1992. **Caroline Caddy**: 'Cosmos' from *Conquistadors*, Penguin, Melbourne, 1991. **Adrian Caesar**: 'Mamma's Cake' from *Hunger Games*, Polonius Press, Cook, ACT, 1996. **Ada Cambridge**: 'An Old Maid's Lament' from *Unspoken Thoughts*, Kegan, Paul, Trench & Co., London, 1887. Reproduced by English Department, University College, UNSW–ADFA, Canberra, 1988. **David Campbell**: 'Town Planning', 'Mothers and Daughters', 'The Australian Dream', and 'Angina' from 'Starting from Central Station' from *Collected Poems* (ed. Leonie J. Kramer), Angus & Robertson, Sydney, 1989. **Lee Cataldi**: 'northshoredirector'sdaughter …' from *Invitation to a Marxist Lesbian Party*, Wild & Woolley, Sydney, 1978; 'kuukuu kardiya and the women who live on the ground (2, 3)' from *The Women Who Live on the Ground*, Penguin, Melbourne, 1990. **Sherryl Clark**: 'Things that Change Us' from *Edge*, Pariah Press, Kew, Vic., 1991. **Elsie Cole**: 'Fenella West' from *Children of Joy*, Lothian Publishing, Melbourne, 1928. **Alison Croggon**: '1 Labour', '2 Hymn', and '3 Cooking' from 'Domestic Art' in *This is the Stone*, Penguin, Melbourne, 1991. **Victor Daley**: 'An Australian Bachelor's Soliloquy' from *Victor Daley* (selected by H.J. Oliver), Angus & Robertson, Sydney, 1963. **Jack Davis**: 'The First-born' from *The First Born and Other Poems*, J.M. Dent, Melbourne, 1970; 'Dingo' from *John Pat and Other Poems*, J.M. Dent, Melbourne, 1988. **Bruce Dawe**: 'Condolences of the Season', 'Drifters', and 'Homecoming' from *Sometimes Gladness*, Longman Cheshire, Melbourne, 1983; 'Some Village-Hampden' from *Towards Sunrise: Poems 1979–1986*, Longman Cheshire, Melbourne, 1986. **Sarah Day**: 'The Christening Dress Comes Airmail' from *A Madder*

Dance, Penguin, Melbourne, 1991. **C.J. Dennis**: 'Uncle Jim' from *The Songs of a Sentimental Bloke*, Angus & Robertson, Sydney, 1915. **Graeme Dixon**: 'To Let' from *Holocaust Island*, University of Queensland Press, St Lucia, 1990. **Rosemary Dobson**: 'Cock Crow' and 'The Major-General' from *Collected Poems*, Angus & Robertson, Sydney, 1991; 'The Apparition' from *Untold Lives: A Sequence of Poems*, Brindabella Press, Canberra, 1992. **Lucy Dougan**: 'My Father in His Thornproof Jacket from Cavan' from *Fremantle Arts Review*, Dec 1993/Jan 1994. **Geoffrey Dutton**: 'A Finished Gentleman' from *New and Selected Poems*, Harper Collins/Angus & Robertson, Sydney, 1993. **Stephen Edgar**: 'Family Portrait' from *Queuing for the Mudd Club*, Twelvetrees, Sandy Bay, Tas., 1985. **Anne Elder**: 'Farmer Goes Berserk' from *Crazy Woman*, Angus & Robertson, Sydney, 1976. **Diane Fahey**: 'Andromache' from *Metamorphoses*, Dangaroo Press, Sydney, 1988; 'Thirteen' © Diane Fahey 1995 reproduced with permission from *The Body in Time* by Diane Fahey, published by Spinifex Press, Melbourne, 1995. **Mary Finnin**: 'Mad Lucy' from *Off Shears*, Hawthorn Press, Melbourne, 1979. **R.D. Fitzgerald**: 'The Wind at Your Door' from *Forty Years' Poems*, Angus & Robertson, Sydney, 1965. **Lionel Fogarty**: 'The Mununjali Exemption Man' from *Munaldjali, Mutuerjaraera: New and Selected Poems*, Hyland House, Melbourne, 1995. **John Forbes**: 'The History of Nostalgia' from *New and Selected Poems*, Harper Collins/Angus & Robertson, Sydney, 1992. **Mabel Forrest**: 'The Cat in the Cupboard' from *Poems*, Cornstalk Publishing Company, Sydney, 1927. **John Foulcher**: 'Pictures from the War' from *Pictures from the War*, Angus & Robertson, Sydney, 1987; 'Skies' from *New and Selected Poems*, Angus & Robertson, Sydney, 1993. **Mary Fullerton**: 'The Grain' and 'The Folk of Brenan's Lane' from *The Breaking Furrow*, Galleon Press, Melbourne, 1921. **Silvana Gardner**: 'Forbidden Language' from *The Painter of Icons*, Boolarong Publications, Brisbane, 1993. **Kevin Gilbert**: 'Memorials' from *Black from the Edge*, Hyland House, Melbourne, 1994. **Barbara Giles**: 'Dans le jardin de mon père, les lilas ont fleuri' and 'Infidel' from *The Hag in the Mirror*, Pariah Press, Kew, Vic., 1989; 'Mama's Little Girl' from *A Savage Coast*, Hale & Iremonger, Sydney, 1993. **Mary**

Gilmore: 'Marri'd', 'War', 'The Square Peg and the Round' and 'Nationality' from *Selected Poems*, ETT Imprint, Sydney, 1998. **Alan Gould**: 'The Chairs of This House' from *The Pausing of the Hours*, Angus & Robertson, Sydney, 1984. **Jamie Grant**: 'Mon Père est Mort' from *The Valley Murders: Poems 1992–95*, William Heinemann, Melbourne, 1995. **Robert Gray**: 'Diptych' from *Skylight*, Angus & Robertson, Sydney, 1984. **Jeff Guess**: 'Present Imperfect' from *Leaving Maps*, Friendly Street Poets, Unley, SA, 1984. **Gillian Hanscombe**: 'A Great Australian Family circa 1960', the author, 1994. **Lesbia Harford**: 'Fatherless' and 'The Wife' from *The Poems of Lesbia Harford* (ed. Drusilla Modjeska and Marjorie Pizer), Sirius/Angus & Robertson, Sydney, 1985. **Charles Harpur**: 'An Aboriginal Mother's Lament' and 'A Man Shall be a Man Yet' from *The Poetical Works of Charles Harpur* (ed. Elizabeth Perkins), Angus & Robertson, Sydney, 1984. **Robert Harris**: 'Forests and Rivers' from *Jane, Interlinear and Other Poems*, Paperbark Press, Sydney, 1992. **Jennifer Harrison**: 'Swan Lake' from *Cabramatta/Cudmirrah*, Black Pepper, North Fitzroy, Vic., 1996. **J.S. Harry**: 'After the Money for the Milk' and 'Mousepoem' from *New and Selected Poems*, Penguin, Melbourne, 1995. **Kevin Hart**: 'The Map', 'Peniel', and 'L'intelligence avec l'ange' from *New and Selected Poems*, Harper Collins/Angus & Robertson, Sydney, 1995. **Gwen Harwood**: 'Monday', 'An Impromptu for Ann Jennings', 'Dialogue', and 'Mother Who Gave Me Life' from *Selected Poems*, ETT Imprint, Sydney, 1997. **Susan Hawthorne**: 'Shell' from *Eat the Ocean* (ed. Liz Murphy), Literary Mouse Press, Perth, 1997. **Jill Hellyer**: 'Living with Aunts' from *Song of the Humpback Whale*, Sisters Publications, Carlton,Vic., 1981. **Kristin Henry**: 'On Learning that Mothers Die' from *One Day She Catches Fire*, Penguin, Melbourne, 1992. **Paul Hetherington**: 'Uncle Bible' from *Shadow Swimmer*, Molongolo Press, Canberra, 1995. **Dorothy Hewett**: 'Legend of the Green Country I–III' and 'Anniversary' from *Collected Poems*, Fremantle Arts Centre Press, Fremantle, 1995. **Philip Hodgins**: 'Shooting the Dogs' from *Down the Lane with Half a Chook*, ABC Enterprises, Sydney, 1988; extract from 'The Way Things Were' in *Animal Warmth*, Angus & Robertson, Sydney, 1990; 'Little Elegies' from *Up on All Fours*,

Harper Collins/Angus & Robertson, Sydney, 1993. **Harry Hooton**: 'Womb to Let' from *Collected Poems*, Harper Collins/Angus & Robertson, Sydney, 1990. **A.D. Hope**: 'Imperial Adam' from *Collected Poems 1930–1970*, Angus & Robertson, Sydney, 1972; 'On an Early Photograph of My Mother' from *A Late Picking*, Angus & Robertson, Sydney, 1975. **Flexmore Hudson**: 'Giovanni Rinaldo, P.O.W.' from *Pools of the Cinnabar Range*, Robertson & Mullens, Melbourne, 1959. **Coral Hull**: 'White Linen at Midnight' from *In the Dog Box of Summer*, Penguin, Melbourne, 1995. **Inez Hyland**: 'Disloyalty' from *In Sunshine and in Shadow*, George Robertson & Co., Melbourne, 1893. **Subhash Jaireth**: 'Brother Anton and Masha' from *Unfinished Poems for Your Violin*, Penguin, Melbourne, 1996. **Kate Jennings**: 'Assassin' from *Cats, Dogs and Pitchforks*, William Heinemann, Melbourne, 1993. **Jill Jones**: 'The Tax Form' from *The Book of Possibilities*, Hale & Iremonger, Sydney, 1997. **Antigone Kefala**: 'Deserted Wife' from *Absence: New and Selected Poems*, Hale & Iremonger, Sydney, 1992. **S.K. Kelen**: 'The House Spider' from *Dingo Sky*, Angus & Robertson, Sydney, 1993. **Aileen Kelly**: 'My Brother's Piano' from *Coming Up for Light*, Pariah Press, Kew, Vic., 1994. **Henry Kendall**: 'In Memoriam Daniel Henry Deniehy' and 'Araluen' from *The Poetical Works of Henry Kendall* (ed. T.T. Reed), Libraries Board of South Australia, Adelaide, 1966. **Jean Kent**: 'A Platform for Legends' from *Verandahs*, Hale & Iremonger, Sydney, 1990. **John Kinsella**: 'The Hay King's Recalcitrant Daughter' from *The Silo*, Fremantle Arts Centre Press, Fremantle, 1995; 'Anathalamion' from *Lightning Tree*, Fremantle Arts Centre Press, Fremantle, 1996. **Peter Kocan**: 'The Little Garrisons' from *Standing with Friends*, William Heinemann, Melbourne, 1992. **Komninos**: 'It's Great to be Mates with a Koori' from *Komninos*, University of Queensland Press, St Lucia, 1991. **Nora Krouk**: 'Post Retirement Blues' from *Faultlines*, Round Table Publications, Ryde, NSW, 1991. **Anthony Lawrence**: 'The Drive' and 'The Custodian of Grief and Wonder' from *The Darkwood Aquarium*, Penguin, 1993. **Henry Lawson**: 'The Fire at Ross's Farm', 'The Babies of Walloon', 'Past Carin'' and 'My Father-in-law and I' from *Collected Verse* (ed. Colin Roderick), Angus &

Robertson, Sydney, 1967–69. **Louisa Lawson:** 'A Pound a Mile' from *The Lonely Crossing*, Dawn Office, Sydney, 1905. **Shelton Lea:** 'And So They've Murdered Julia's Lawn' from *Poems from a Peach Melba Hat*, Abalone, Cheltenham, Vic., 1985. **Joyce Lee:** 'My Father's Country' from *Plain Dreaming*, Pariah Press, Kew, Vic., 1992. **Geoffrey Lehmann:** 'Pieces for My Father (IV)', 'The Flight of Children', and 'Menindee' from *Collected Poems*, William Heinemann, Melbourne, 1997. **Tony Lintermans:** 'The Shed Manifesto' from *The Shed Manifesto*, Scribe, 1989. **Kate Llewellyn:** 'Divorce' from *Crosshatched*, Harper Collins/Angus & Robertson, Sydney, 1994. **Myron Lysenko:** 'Pets & Death & Indoor Plants' from *Pets & Death & Indoor Plants*, Penguin, Melburne, 1991. **James McAuley:** 'Pietà', 'Numbers and Makes', and 'Because' from *Collected Poems 1936–1970*, Angus & Robertson, Sydney, 1971. **Ronald McCuaig:** 'Au Tombeau de Mon Père' from *Selected Poems*, Harper Collins/Angus & Robertson, Sydney, 1992. **Nan McDonald:** 'The Hatters' from *The Lighthouse and Other Poems*, Angus & Robertson, Sydney, 1959. **Kenneth Mackenzie:** 'A Fairy Tale' from *The Poems of Kenneth Mackenzie* (ed. Evan Jones), Angus & Robertson, Sydney, 1972. **Rhyll McMaster:** 'Washing the Money' and 'Holiday House' from *Washing the Money*, Angus & Robertson, Sydney, 1986; 'Lost' from 'My Mother and I Become Victims of a Stroke' in *On My Empty Feet*, William Heinemann, Melbourne, 1993. **Jennifer Maiden:** 'In the Caesura' from *The Winter Baby*, Angus & Robertson, Sydney, 1990; 'Plastic Ponies' from *Acoustic Shadow*, Penguin, Melbourne, 1993. **David Malouf:** 'The Year of the Foxes' from *Bicycle and Other Poems*, University of Queensland Press, St Lucia, 1970. **Philip Martin:** 'Nursing Home' from *A Flag for the Wind: New and Selected Poems*, Longman Cheshire, Melbourne, 1988. **Joan Mas:** 'The Widow' from *The Fear and the Flowering*, Edwards & Shaw, Sydney, 1975. **James Michael:** extract from 'John Cumberland' from *John Cumberland*, J. R. Clarke, Sydney, 1860. **Mal Morgan:** 'Arthur Mee' from *Throwaway Moon: New and Selected Poems*, Hyland House, Melbourne, 1995. **Mudrooroo:** 'Song One' from *The Garden of Gethsemane: Poems from the Lost Decade*, Hyland House, Melbourne, 1991. **Nina Murdoch:** 'Socks' from *Songs of the Open*

Air, William Brooks & Co., Sydney, 1915. **Les Murray**: 'Evening Alone at Bunyah' and 'The Mitchells' from *Collected Poems*, Harper Collins/Angus & Robertson, Sydney, 1991; 'Home Suite' from *Translations from the Natural World*, Isabella Press, Paddington, NSW, 1992. **John Shaw Neilson**: 'Marian's Child', 'Polly and Dad and the Spring Cart', and 'The Vixen has Spoken' from *John Shaw Neilson: Poetry, Autobiography and Correspondence* (ed. Cliff Hanna), University of Queensland Press, St Lucia, 1991. **Vera Newsom**: 'Sligo' from *Midnight Snow*, Hale & Iremonger, Sydney, 1988; 'My Grandmother Singing' from *The Apple and the Serpent*, Hale & Iremonger, Sydney, 1992. **Oodgeroo Noonuccal**: 'Ballad of the Totems' and 'Colour Bar' from *My People*, Jacaranda Press, Brisbane, 1970. **Mark O'Connor**: 'The Dance Floor in the Cave–Kanangra Walls' from *Poetry of the Mountains*, Second Back Row Press, Leura, NSW, 1988. **Jan Owen**: 'Freud and the Vacuum Cleaner' from *Boy with a Telescope*, Angus & Robertson, Sydney, 1986. **Geoff Page**: 'My Mother's God' from *Selected Poems*, Harper Collins/Angus & Robertson, Sydney, 1991; 'Middle Names' from *Gravel Corners*, Harper Collins/Angus & Robertson, Sydney, 1992. **A.B. Paterson**: 'The Man Who was Away' and 'A Bush Christening' from *The Collected Verse of A.B. Paterson*, Angus & Robertson, Sydney, 1921. **Tom Petsinis**: extract from *Inheritance*, Penguin, Melbourne, 1995. **πO**: 'The Women' from *The Fitzroy Poems*, Collective Effort Press, Melbourne, 1989. **Dorothy Porter**: 'My Mother', 'My Daughter', and 'My Sleeping Brother' from *Akhenaten*, University of Queensland Press, St Lucia, 1992. **Peter Porter**: 'Somme and Flanders' and 'Family Album' from *Collected Poems*, Oxford University Press, UK, 1983; 'Where We Came In' from *Fast Forward*, Oxford University Press, UK, 1984; 'The Second Husband' from *The Chair of Babel*, Oxford University Press, UK, 1992. **Wendy Poussard**: 'Telegram from Grandmother' from *Ground Truth*, Pariah Press, Kew, Vic., 1987. **Craig Powell**: 'It Used to be Different' from *I Learn by Going*, South Head Press, Sydney, 1968. **Jennifer Rankin**: 'Daub Wall' and 'Poem for David' from *Collected Poems* (ed. Judith Rodriguez), University of Queensland Press, St Lucia, 1990. **Vicki Raymond**: 'Small Arm Practice' from *Small Arm Practice*, William Heinemann, London,

1989. **Barrett Reid**: 'Marie at Saint-Cloud' from *Making Country*, Harper Collins/Angus & Robertson in association with Paperbark Press, Sydney, 1995. **David Reiter**: 'Cats Slip In' from *Changing House*, Jacaranda Press, Brisbane, 1991. **Elizabeth Riddell**: 'News of a Baby' and 'Suburban Evening' from *Selected Poems*, Harper Collins/Angus & Robertson, Sydney; 'The Other Face' from *The Difficult Island*, Molongolo Press, Canberra, 1994. **Judith Rodriguez**: 'Eskimo Occasion' and 'An Upbringing' from *New and Selected Poems*, University of Queensland Press, St Lucia, 1988; 'Cordelia's Music for Lear', the *Age*, 1994. **Peter Rose**: 'The Living Archive' from *The Catullan Rag*, Picador, Sydney, 1993. **David Rowbotham**: 'The Bus-stop on the Somme' from *New and Selected Poems*, Penguin, Melbourne, 1994. **J.R. Rowland**: 'Family Happiness' from *Snow and Other Poems*, Angus & Robertson, Sydney, 1971. **Graham Rowlands**: from *Jeremy's Poems*: 'The Curls' from *Southerly* and 'The Hypocrite' from *Going Down Swinging*. **Tracy Ryan**: 'Morningswood' from *Killing Delilah*, Fremantle Arts Centre Press, Fremantle, 1994; 'Exegesis' from *Bluebeard in Drag*, Fremantle Arts Centre Press, Fremantle, 1996. **Philip Salom**: 'Benchleys' from *The Projectionist*, Fremantle Arts Centre Press, Fremantle, 1983; 'Train Talk: The Three of Us' from *Feeding the Ghost*, Penguin, Melbourne, 1993. **John A. Scott**: 'The Passing, at Boho' from *Singles*, University of Queensland Press, St Lucia, 1989. **Margaret Scott**: 'Settlers' Graveyard' from *Visited*, Angus & Robertson, Sydney, 1983; 'Making Redcurrant Jelly' from 'Housework' in *The Black Swans*, Angus & Robertson, Sydney, 1988. **Tom Shapcott**: 'Black Cat' from 'Instructions for Moving' from *Selected Poems 1968–1988*, University of Queensland Press, St Lucia, 1988; 'Ripe Bananas' from *The City of Home*, University of Queensland Press, St Lucia, 1995. **Jemal Sharah**: 'The Lares' from *Path of Ghosts*, William Heinemann, Melbourne, 1994. **R.A. Simpson**: 'The Telephone's Working Again' from *Selected Poems*, University of Queensland Press, St Lucia, 1981. **Alex Skovron**: 'Beyond Nietzsche' from *Sleeve Notes*, Hale & Iremonger, Sydney, 1992. **Peter Skrzynecki**: 'Feliks Skrzynecki' and 'Kornelia Woloszczuk' from *Immigrant Chronicle*, University of Queensland Press, St Lucia, 1975. **Kenneth Slessor**: 'Five Visions of Captain

Cook V', *Poems*, Angus & Robertson, Sydney, 1963. **Vivian Smith**: 'At an Exhibition of Historical Pictures, Hobart' from *An Island South*, Angus & Robertson, Sydney, 1967; 'For My Daughter' from *Selected Poems*, Angus & Robertson, Sydney, 1985. **Edith Speers**: 'Open Letter to an Ex-defacto Postnuptial Cannibal' from *By Way of a Vessel*, Twelvetrees, Sandy Bay, Tas., 1986. **Nicolette Stasko**: 'Keepers' from *Black Night with Windows*, Angus & Robertson, Sydney, 1994. **Jennifer Strauss**: 'Models' from *Winter Driving*, Sisters Publications, Carlton South, Vic., 1981; 'A Mother's Day Letter: Not for Posting' from *Tierra del Fuego: New and Selected Poems*, Pariah Press, Kew, Vic., 1997. **Bobbi Sykes**: 'Miscegenation' from *Eclipse*, University of Queensland Press, St Lucia, 1996. **Andrew Taylor:** 'The Dead Father' from *Selected Poems*, University of Queensland Press, St Lucia, 1988. **Ian Templeman:** 'My Father's Letter' from *These Glimpsed Interiors*, Molongolo Press, Canberra, 1997. **Michael Thwaites**: 'Coming into the Clyde' from *The Honey Man*, Aslan Publications, Braddon, ACT, 1993. **John Tranter:** 'Backyard' from *Under Berlin*, University of Queensland Press, St Lucia, 1988. **Dimitris Tsaloumas:** 'Reffo' from 'Rhapsodic Meditation on the Melbourne Suburb of St Kilda' in *The Barge*, University of Queensland Press, St Lucia, 1993. **Louise Wakeling**: 'The Water and the Wine', the author, 1994. **Lyndon Walker:** 'Dinner' from *Singers and Winners*, Pariah Press, Kew, Vic., 1984. **Chris Wallace-Crabbe:** 'An Elegy' and 'The Inheritance' from *For Crying Out Loud*, Oxford University Press, UK, 1990; 'Trace Elements' from *Rungs of Time*, Oxford University Press, UK, 1993. **Alan Wearne:** 'Lorraine McNab ...' from 'Out There' in *New Devil, New Parish*, University of Queensland Press, St Lucia, 1976. **Stephen J. Williams:** 'Flowers for the Dead' from *The Ninth Satire*, Pariah Press, Kew, Vic., 1993. **Judith Wright:** 'Two Dreamtimes' and 'For a Pastoral Family' from *A Human Pattern: Selected Poems*, ETT Imprint, Sydney, 1996. **Warwick Wynne**: 'Tractor and Father and Child' from *The Colour of Maps*, Five Islands Press, Wollongong, 1995. **Fay Zwicky:** 'Father in a Mirror' from 'Four Poems from America', 'Domestic Architecture',

'Breathing Exercises', and 'Letting Go' from *Poems 1970–92*, University of Queensland Press, St Lucia, 1992.

Every effort has been made to trace the original source of copyright material contained in this book. The publisher would be pleased to hear from copyright holders to rectify any errors or omissions.

INDEX OF THEMES

This index is intended to provide a guide to some dominant themes that emerged as poems were selected. An initial attempt to provide cross-referencing to do justice to the fact that many poems could have appeared in several categories had to be abandoned because the index was becoming impractically cumbersome. The entries therefore represent a choice of one theme or preoccupation as dominant, but the possibility that other poems could be slotted into almost every category should be borne in mind when the index is used. For instance, Judith Beveridge's 'Child Fishing' could, like Peter Skrzynecki's 'Feliks Skrzynecki', be entered under parent–child relationships; Jack Davis's 'Dingo' could be under Australia as home; Bobbi Sykes's 'Miscegenation' could be under dysfunctional families. The index is a rough guide only to the richness of the collection.

INDEX OF POETS AND TITLES

INDEX OF FIRST LINES